MACMILLAN MASTER GUIDES
THE WIFE OF BATH'S TALE
BY GEOFFREY CHAUCER

NICHOLAS MARSH

MACMILLAN

First published 1987 by
MACMILLAN PRESS LTD
Houndmills, Basingstoke, Hampshire RG21 6XS
and London
Companies and representatives
throughout the world

ISBN 0–333–42229–5

A catalogue record for this book is available
from the British Library.

11 10 9 8 7 6 5 4
05 04 03 02 01 00 99 98 97

Printed in Malaysia

MACMILLAN MASTER GUIDES

GENERAL EDITOR: JAMES GIBSON

JANE AUSTEN	*Emma* Norman Page
	Sense and Sensibility Judy Simons
	Persuasion Judy Simons
	Pride and Prejudice Raymond Wilson
	Mansfield Park Richard Wirdnam
SAMUEL BECKETT	*Waiting for Godot* Jennifer Birkett
WILLIAM BLAKE	*Songs of Innocence* and *Songs of Experience* Alan Tomlinson
ROBERT BOLT	*A Man for All Seasons* Leonard Smith
CHARLOTTE BRONTË	*Jane Eyre* Robert Miles
EMILY BRONTË	*Wuthering Heights* Hilda D. Spear
JOHN BUNYAN	*The Pilgrim's Progress* Beatrice Batson
GEOFFREY CHAUCER	*The Miller's Tale* Michael Alexander
	The Pardoner's Tale Geoffrey Lester
	The Wife of Bath's Tale Nicholas Marsh
	The Knight's Tale Anne Samson
	The Prologue to the Canterbury Tales Nigel Thomas and Richard Swan
JOSEPH CONRAD	*The Secret Agent* Andrew Mayne
CHARLES DICKENS	*Bleak House* Dennis Butts
	Great Expectations Dennis Butts
	Hard Times Norman Page
GEORGE ELIOT	*Middlemarch* Graham Handley
	Silas Marner Graham Handley
	The Mill on the Floss Helen Wheeler
T.S. ELIOT	*Murder in the Cathedral* Paul Lapworth
	Selected Poems Andrew Swarbrick
HENRY FIELDING	*Joseph Andrews* Trevor Johnson
E.M. FORSTER	*A Passage to India* Hilda D. Spear
	Howards End Ian Milligan
WILLIAM GOLDING	*The Spire* Rosemary Sumner
	Lord of the Flies Raymond Wilson
OLIVER GOLDSMITH	*She Stoops to Conquer* Paul Ranger
THOMAS HARDY	*The Mayor of Casterbridge* Ray Evans
	Tess of the d'Urbervilles James Gibson
	Far from the Madding Crowd Colin Temblett-Wood
BEN JONSON	*Volpone* Michael Stout
JOHN KEATS	*Selected Poems* John Garrett
RUDYARD KIPLING	*Kim* Leonée Ormond
PHILIP LARKIN	*The Less Deceived* and *The Whitsun Weddings* Andrew Swarbrick

MACMILLAN MASTER GUIDES

D. H. LAWRENCE · *Sons and Lovers* · R. P. Draper

HARPER LEE · *To Kill a Mockingbird* · Jean Armstrong

LAURIE LEE · *Cider with Rosie* · Brian Tarbitt

GERARD MANLEY HOPKINS · *Selected Poems* · R. J. C. Watt

CHRISTOPHER MARLOWE · *Doctor Faustus* · David A. Male

THE METAPHYSICAL POETS · Joan van Emden

THOMAS MIDDLETON and WILLIAM ROWLEY · *The Changeling* · Tony Bromham

ARTHUR MILLER · *The Crucible* · Leonard Smith
Death of a Salesman · Peter Spalding

GEORGE ORWELL · *Animal Farm* · Jean Armstrong

WILLIAM SHAKESPEARE · *Richard II* · Charles Barber
Othello · Tony Bromham
Hamlet · Jean Brooks
King Lear · Francis Casey
Henry V · Peter Davison
The Winter's Tale · Diana Devlin
Julius Caesar · David Elloway
Macbeth · David Elloway
The Merchant of Venice · A. M. Kinghorn
Measure for Measure · Mark Lilly
Henry IV Part I · Helen Morris
Romeo and Juliet · Helen Morris
A Midsummer Night's Dream · Kenneth Pickering
The Tempest · Kenneth Pickering
Coriolanus · Gordon Williams
Antony and Cleopatra · Martin Wine

GEORGE BERNARD SHAW · *St Joan* · Leonée Ormond

RICHARD SHERIDAN · *The School for Scandal* · Paul Ranger
The Rivals · Jeremy Rowe

ALFRED TENNYSON · *In Memoriam* · Richard Gill

EDWARD THOMAS · *Selected Poems* · Gerald Roberts

ANTHONY TROLLOPE · *Barchester Towers* · K. M. Newton

JOHN WEBSTER · *The White Devil* and *The Duchess of Malfi* · David A. Male

VIRGINIA WOOLF · *To the Lighthouse* · John Mepham
Mrs Dalloway · Julian Pattison

WILLIAM WORDSWORTH · *The Prelude Books I and II* · Helen Wheeler

CONTENTS

GENERAL EDITOR'S PREFACE

The aim of the Macmillan Master Guides is to help you to appreciate the book you are studying by providing information about it and by suggesting ways of reading and thinking about it which will lead to a fuller understanding. The section on the writer's life and background has been designed to illustrate those aspects of the writer's life which have influenced the work, and to place it in its personal and literary context. The summaries and critical commentary are of special importance in that each brief summary of the action is followed by an examination of the significant critical points. The space which might have been given to repetitive explanatory notes has been devoted to a detailed analysis of the kind of passage which might confront you in an examination. Literary criticism is concerned with both the broader aspects of the work being studied and with its detail. The ideas which meet us in reading a great work of literature, and their relevance to us today, are an essential part of our study, and our Guides look at the thought of their subject in some detail. But just as essential is the craft with which the writer has constructed his work of art, and this may be considered under several technical headings – characterisation, language, style and stagecraft, for example.

The authors of these Guides are all teachers and writers of wide experience, and they have chosen to write about books they admire and know well in the belief that they can communicate their admiration to you. But you yourself must read and know intimately the book you are studying. No one can do that for you. You should see this book as a lamp-post. Use it to shed light, not to lean against. If you know your text and know what it is saying about life, and how it says it, then you will enjoy it, and there is no better way of passing an examination in literature.

JAMES GIBSON

ACKNOWLEDGEMENTS

The author and publishers wish to thank the following who has kindly given permission for the use of copyright material: Oxford University Press for extracts from *The Works of Geoffrey Chaucer*, 2nd edition, ed. F. N. Robinson, 1957.

Cover illustration: a detail from the *Luttrell Psalter*; margin illustration showing a wife beating her husband with a distoff. Photograph © British Library, London and by courtesy of the Bridgeman Art Library.

1 THE RELIGIOUS AND SOCIAL BACKGROUND

1.1 CHAUCER IN A TIME OF CHANGE

Geoffrey Chaucer wrote a long time ago, but we must not think of his poetry as 'old'. He was an innovator in his time: his poetry was the first serious metrical verse in English, and was full of original and provocative ideas. Also, he lived at a time of social, political and religious upheaval, a time of rapid change as volatile as the twentieth century. Looking at the turmoil of the fourteenth century, we will be able to see how Chaucer weaves together the conflicting threads of his time, making a complex reality that is entirely his own. This is the context in which we must understand 'The Wife of Bath's Prologue and Tale', so some explanation of Chaucer's life and the major developments of his time is necessary.

Chaucer's life

Chaucer must have been born in about 1340, although the exact date of his birth is not known. His father, John Chaucer, had connections with the wine trade and in 1348 he was appointed to be Deputy to the King's Butler at Southampton. He married Agnes de Copton at some time after 1328, and she is presumed to be the poet's mother. Geoffrey Chaucer's childhood was spent in London and it is thought that he attended St Paul's Almonry for his early schooling. His family was comfortably well-to-do, but they were not 'gentry'.

At some time in the early 1350s a place was found for the young Geoffrey as a page in the household of Lionel, later Duke of Clarence, one of the sons of Edward III. This was a very good position for a hopeful boy, bringing him into contact with refined court manners and enabling him to meet many of the great nobility and royalty. At this time he must have met the Duke of Lancaster, John of Gaunt, his most loyal patron and protector.

Chaucer quickly gained promotion to positions of trust. In 1359 he was sent to the French wars and was captured near Rheims. King Edward III himself paid part of the ransom, and by 1367 we hear that Chaucer was in the king's own household. Around the same year he married Philippa de Roet, a lady in attendance on the queen and sister-in-law of John of Gaunt. We know hardly anything of their life together or of their feelings for each other, but there can be no doubt that Chaucer's connection to the influential de Roet family was advantageous to his career. He was trusted with a succession of diplomatic and trading missions abroad, and was appointed Controller of Customs in the Port of London in 1374, Justice of the Peace for Kent in 1385, and Knight of the Shire in 1386.

In the same year, however, he was suddenly deprived of his offices, probably because of John of Gaunt was out of the country, for he was restored to favour on his patron's return in 1389. In the meantime, during 1387, his wife Philippa died. These three troubled years are almost certainly the time when he began work on *The Canterbury Tales*, the ambitious poem that was his main occupation, outside intermittent official duties, for several years. We do not know when he abandoned it, unfinished, but in the 1390s he felt that he was growing old, and complained that poetry no longer came easily to him. In this last decade of his life Chaucer's income was reasonable, but he is known to have been often in debt, and must have felt more secure in 1399 when Gaunt's son Henry Bolingbroke came to the throne and gave the poet an additional pension of twenty marks a year. Chaucer did not enjoy this security for long, however: he died on 25 October 1400, and was buried in Westminster Abbey.

Major developments of the time

In 1348–9 and in 1361 the bubonic plague ravaged England. The scale of the great plagues is difficult to imagine; in some parts of the country they killed almost everybody, while in England as a whole something more than thirty per cent of the population died. The effect of a disaster on this scale is hard to envisage: everybody saw the potent images of death, infected houses being burned, carts full of corpses and the pits used as mass common graves. Everyone lost either friends or relatives. Medieval society believed in Providence: everything that happened was God's will, and it is not surprising therefore that the plagues were thought to have been sent by God as a warning of coming judgement, like the biblical Flood. The response of many people was to turn with new energy to reform, stamping out corruption and striving with new urgency for a good society.

A movement attacking corruption in the Church was inspired by John Wycliffe, an Oxford scholar whose writings and preachings questioned the authority of the pope and the clergy. He denounced corrupt practices in the Church and suggested the idea of a conscience, a sense of right and wrong which could be judged by the individual. Wycliffe also began to translate the Bible into English so that ordinary people could more easily understand the scriptures. Wycliffe himself seems to have had faults as a reformer: he held livings where he was not resident, for example, and he pursued a self-interested career in the Church for much of his life. Nor did he organise a 'movement' as such, for his followers were largely learned Oxford scholars and the controversy over his works was a scholarly affair. Nevertheless his ideas achieved some publicity, while many poorer priests and itinerant clerks followed his doctrines and spread the reforming zeal. Wycliffites and reforming clergy were given the name 'Lollards', and in Chaucer's time they were a significant influence all over England. Many of the virtuous traits of 'Lollardry' are incorporated into the honest Parson of *The Canterbury Tales*, who eschews personal gain and whose particular virtue is in setting a good example of humility and hard work to his flock.

The plagues accelerated economic changes too, by bringing about a shortage of labour which enhanced the power of serfs and enabled them to gain new freedoms to better their lot. In this volatile situation, a rebellion took place. The Peasants' Revolt of 1381 was apparently an expression of anger at poverty and injustice, and desire for greater freedom, that flared simultaneously in several counties and spread quickly to most areas of south-east England. Several groups of rebels converged on London, and the young King Richard II had to negotiate with them in order to disperse the mobs and save his capital. Among the leaders of this revolt were three whose names are still remembered: Wat Tyler, John Bull and Jack Straw. Although by modern revolutionary standards the Peasants' Revolt was a minor episode without any hope of overthrowing feudal government, it was a startling sign of people's new aspirations, and of the vulnerability of all old certainties in a fast-changing land.

Chaucer himself travelled widely through Europe. He saw active service, was taken prisoner and ransomed in 1359–60, and probably served in Picardy with Lancaster in 1369. He was also sent abroad on several diplomatic missions, travelling to France in 1368, 1377 and 1387; and to Italy twice, in 1372–3 and 1378. He was an avid reader and quickly absorbed the new writings and ideas he found in France and Italy. In particular he read widely in the French courtly tradition and translated Jean de Meun and Guillaume de Loris's *Roman de la Rose* into English. He also read the works of Dante and Boccaccio. On the Continent at that time a new culture was being born. The Church's stranglehold on art and thought was being weakened by renewed interest in the pagan cultures of ancient Greece and Rome, and the rapid progress of trade and exploration encouraged an exciting climate in which democratic ideas and social criticisms flourished. Chaucer, in effect, travelled into the European Renaissance and brought many exciting ideas and attitudes back with him to England.

The English court was also changing, becoming increasingly conscious of fashion after the accession of the child-king Richard II in 1377. The court's extravagance under Richard was a matter of concern to Parliament while he was still only a boy. Court ceremony increased, with a greater emphasis on elaborate dress and affected manners. This atmosphere encouraged the English to import fashions and artistic forms from the Continent. In 'The General Prologue' the contrast between the Knight and the Squire shows us that a generation gap existed as great as that, say, between a parent in the 1960s and his hippy children; and the absurd imitation of court pomp by the guildsmen and their wives, also described in 'The General Prologue', shows the formative influence of the court on town society.

Social historians point to the rapid growth of trade as increasing communication between different parts of Europe at this time, and accelerating the spread of new attitudes. Growing trade swelled the ranks of the new urban commercial class – the bourgeoisie – while there was an accompanying decline in the value of land. The economic power of the traditional gentry, whose wealth was in their vast estates, was undermined. One of the clearest examples of the new middle class among the Canterbury pilgrims is the Franklin. He is described as a tradesman who used commercial success to buy an estate, and held influential offices as magistrate and sheriff in his area, where he set up to live as a gentleman. What we now call 'social mobility' was relatively new in Chaucer's time, but its growth was very rapid. Understandably, the rigid structures of Church and feudal state began to disintegrate in face of these mounting pressures for reform and change.

1.2 ALTERNATIVE VIEWS OF THE WORLD

'Old certainties' and 'new' attitudes were mentioned in Section 1.1 but, in fact, these two conflicting views of the world existed side by side. It is important to remember, however, that life is always more complex than any system of thought: the aim of this section is merely to focus on the main opposing ideas, hoping these will help to explain some of the subtleties that appear in 'The Wife of Bath's Prologue and Tale'. We can call these old and new attitudes to life 'medieval' and 'modern' respectively.

The medieval view

In the medieval view of the world, every creature and thing had a purpose and a pre-ordained place. The cause of all purpose and order was God. He presided over a spiritual edifice through his 'vicar' on earth, the pope, and all religious matters were under the authority of the Roman Church. God also presided over a secular edifice through his 'viceroy' on earth, the king, whose family was originally chosen and anointed, and who therefore held a divine right to rule over all other members of society. This is, of course, a simplified picture of medieval thought, but the main point is clear: the authority of pope and king, and the two hierarchical structures they controlled, could not be questioned. A consequence of seeing every person fitted into a rigid social structure was that individuals were not seen as important. Private hopes and despairs were thought to be insignificant in comparison to the grand 'order' in which they held either an exalted or lowly place. It can be difficult for a modern student to understand how trivial an individual's feelings seemed in the medieval world. Modern thought pays attention to the individual: his romantic ecstasy or his suicidal despair. A good example of the medieval attitude occurs near the end of Chaucer's *Troilus and Criseyde*. The story of Troilus's tragic passion is over. When he dies, his perspective on life changes completely and his soul sees the world from the 'medieval' point of view for the first time. Troilus rises to the stars where he hears 'sownes ful of hevenyssh melodye':

> And down from thennes faste he gan avyse
> This litel spot of erthe, that with the se
> Embraced is, and fully gan despise
> This wrecched world, and held al vanite
> To respect of the pleyn felicite
> That is in hevene above.

(*The Complete Works of Geoffrey Chaucer*, (ed.) F. N. Robinson, (1957) p.479)

In literature, one consequence of this rigidly ordered view of the world was the schematic development of characters. People were not eccentric or unique individuals, like the characters we find in the novels of Charles Dickens or D. H. Lawrence. Instead, they were described as types, and often they had some particular moral significance. An enormously fat man with glittering avaricious eyes, for example, would represent the sin of gluttony; or the character Piers in William Langland's *Piers the Plowman* stands for honesty and hard work. Characters like these, who show little individuality and whose importance is in the sins or virtues they represent, are called allegorical; and Chaucer's audience would recognise the stock figures from the way they were described. Chaucer often drew on this fund of stock figures, although as we will see, his characters' individuality develops far beyond the limits of contemporary conventions.

More complicated and precise definitions of character could be drawn from the intricacies of astrology. A mass of information about someone's character is gained from working out their horoscope: the influences of various planets in different conjunctions with each other give scope for wide and complex variations in characterisation. Chaucer refers to astrology frequently in *The Canterbury Tales*, and we will discuss the Wife of Bath's horoscope in some detail during the general commentary on the text.

A second ready-made system for analysing characters was medieval medicine. There were thought to be four 'humours' or natural juices in the body, and in a healthy person these fluids were supposed to be present in balanced quantities. Any excess of one or another fluid, it was thought, led to illness. Each 'humour' was associated with two qualities and with one of the four elements of which all matter was thought to be composed: earth, air, fire or water. In theory, each person held a natural slight excess of one or another humour, and this determined their dominant humour or their character. Medical beliefs were also associated with planets and colours, so here again we find a complicated scheme able to express subtle variations of character within its all-embracing order. For example, the Wife of Bath's portrait in 'The General Prologue' describes her as 'reed of hewe', and her 'hosen weren of fyn scarlet reed'. Chaucer's audience would immediately recognise these signs of a 'sanguine' or blood-dominated type, and would deduce the Wife's quick temper and strong but inconstant feelings from what they already knew of the typical 'sanguine' character. The science of physiognomy, or reading character from facial features, was also related to astrology and medicine, so we will find the Wife of Bath pointing out that she was 'gat-tothed' and expecting the pilgrims to understand this as a sign of lechery, then referring to a birth-mark as 'the prente of seinte Venus seel', by way of further astrological proof.

Further details relevant to the Wife are discussed in the general commentary. The main point to understand now is that characterisation, from a medieval point of view, was a complicated system evolved to describe the variety between human beings; but we must never quite forget that this system relied on a rigid framework of beliefs. Ultimately, religious and moral order, and royal and papal authority, bounded everything the medieval person saw or felt: everybody and everything had its place. We will see that the Wife of Bath's place is very carefully defined in these terms; and however much we may be tempted, in our modern way, to excuse her or even to take her side, we must never ignore the medieval view of her that Chaucer is at pains to reveal in her Prologue and Tale.

The modern view

The modern way of looking at the world requires less explanation since it is essentially the same attitude that prevails today. However, a few points help to bring out the contrast between modern and medieval attitudes. First, when we think about a character our main interest lies in what makes that person unique: their eccentricities or individuality rather than their classification into types. We are fascinated by people's dreams, hopes, loves and hates; and we interpret irrational actions in terms of tension, emotional stress, or by using modern psychology's idea of the subconscious. The details and variants are not important to us now; the main point is that we believe in the value, sensitivity and significance of individual people. This contrasts with the medieval point of view which sees the world and all man's concerns as 'vanite'.

From the modern point of view everything else follows from the importance of the individual. We believe that the cleverest and greatest people rise to the highest positions; a hard-working man will make a lot of money. All through our upbringing we are told: 'It depends on *you*; if you want to be a lawyer, doctor or president, go out and do your best: it's up to *you*'. In this way we underline our belief that the social and moral order of the world is determined by human individuality; and in our literary characters we celebrate the inner lives of individuals. This is directly opposed to the medieval God-centred view.

Chaucer's originality

In seeking to understand Chaucer we must take an unbiased attitude
to these opposing philosophies. We tend to think, patronisingly, that
a medieval serf had no idea of equality. It is salutary to look at the
other side of the question as well. How many modern young people
really can go out to become doctors, lawyers and presidents? This,
surely, is just as much an illusion as the medieval belief that serfs
were born inferior. Chaucer's mind is capacious enough to see the
truth and falsehood in both medieval and modern outlooks; and his
originality lies in his ability to weave and blend elements of both
views together. In this way he creates a complex reality that provokes
thought and does not give facile answers to the problems of life. It is
from this standpoint, that sees a much more complicated reality than
either single view could express, that we should approach 'The Wife
of Bath's Prologue and Tale'.

1.3 CHANGING TIMES AND TWO MAJOR THEMES OF THE WIFE OF BATH'S PROLOGUE AND TALE

The Wife of Bath raises two major issues: sexual and love relationships within marriage, and the quality of nobility that she calls
'gentillesse'.

Love and marriage

In Chaucer's time there were two predominant ways of viewing
relations between the sexes. First, the institution of marriage was not
confused with romantic feelings as it is now. It was an unquestioned
part of the social and religious order, and it was there for social and
financial security, and for procreation. Alison of Bath was first
married when she was twelve years old; her husband was a rich old
man. This was an explicit bargain: her youth, beauty and fertility
were traded for his money. Alison's family would also have taken
into account that the groom was likely to die of old age quite quickly.
Such crass trading in young girls as wife-slaves would not shock
Chaucer's audience: it was simply part of the accepted order of
society. In addition, marriage gave the husband almost unlimited
power over his wife. She was his property to do with as he
liked – though this could vary according to the power of her family
and their ability to protect her.

On the other hand, ideas of 'courtly love' had gained some prominence and fashion in Chaucer's time, popularised in courtly romances imported from France, including Chaucer's own translation *The Romaunt of the Rose*. The courtly lover is a type we recognise more easily in the present day. His love for his lady is a kind of adoring worship, but he feels himself so unworthy that he falls ill and, in theory, will die in despair if she does not take pity on him. If she shows pity, he then dares to offer his 'servyse', and undertakes battles and tasks for her. At this stage she may begin to feel that he is 'worthy', and if he shows himself steadfastly loyal and deserving, this may kindle her love and lead her to grant him her favour. Historians still argue about how much influence 'courtly love' had on day-to-day manners in medieval times. However, the supposed courts of love presided over by Eleanour of Aquitaine and Marie of Champagne in twelfth-century Poitiers gained legendary fame, and 'courtly' literature spread and grew.

We can distinguish certain clearly 'modern' characteristics in courtly love. First, the individual's emotions are indulged and become more important than life or death. Second, the lover's worship is woman-centred: she becomes a faultless idol, taking the place of God. This system also directly contradicts both the man's authority in marriage – for in 'courtly love' the woman has authority – and its own idealism. 'Courtly love' is a paradoxical ideal, for with all the worship and exaltation of womanhood, the ultimate aim of the lover is to possess and so conquer her. We will hear much more of these conflicts and paradoxes about love when we look at the Wife's Prologue and Tale in detail.

Gentillesse

The theme of 'gentillesse' is developed in 'The Wife of Bath's Prologue and Tale' as a debate between old and new values. There is no modern equivalent of the word 'gentillesse', but 'nobility' and 'virtue' between them give an idea of its meaning. The traditional view was that 'gentillesse' was inherited, so the more 'gentil' your family, the higher you were born in the social scale, the greater your nobility and virtue would be. This fits the medieval view of an ordered society with social ranks rigidly fixed and superiority passed down through heredity by some divine law of natural distinction. The modern view, argued by the old woman in 'The Wife of Bath's Tale', is that 'gentillesse' is a quality of noble goodness that people show by living good lives. She argues that 'gentillesse' can be found equally among rich and poor, for virtue comes from God, not our parents. You can see at once how much more contemporary and democratic this view is, and how it fits the new attitudes I have already discussed.

These major issues will be examined at length in the commentary. The main thing to remember as we begin the study of Chaucer is the context of social and religious upheaval in which he wrote. We must seek to understand the medieval world-view as a valid system of established belief, and guard against falsifying Chaucer's subtle creation by simplifying or 'modernising' his characters and ideas.

2 THE CANTERBURY TALES

2.1 'THE GENERAL PROLOGUE'

'The General Prologue' provides the frame for all the Canterbury Tales. In the middle of April, spring revives the land, and thirty travellers meet by chance at the Tabard Inn in Southwark, near London. They are pilgrims on their way to the shrine of St Thomas à Becket, who was murdered in Canterbury cathedral in 1170. They decide to travel together, and the host of the Tabard, Harry Bailey, makes a suggestion: they will each tell two stories on the way to Canterbury and another two on the way back. They will be ruled by him and he will decide the order in which they tell their stories. Afterwards, he will judge who has told the best story, and the winner of this competition will have a free supper at the Tabard on their return. If they agree to these terms, Harry Bailey says he will go with them on the journey and pay his own expenses. The thirty pilgrims agree to the suggestion, and next morning they all ride out together on the first stage of their journey to Canterbury.

Certain other points about 'The General Prologue' are useful to know. First, Chaucer emphasises that the journey has two motives: it is both a spring holiday for pleasure, and a religious pilgrimage to the martyr's shrine. The opening lines describe how nature comes alive and overflows with procreative energy in the spring, and link this with renewed sensual energy in mankind: 'Thanne longen folk to goon on pilgrimages'. The word 'corage' is used to denote the sexual energy of birds in the mating season, and occurs again to underline the pilgrims' dual motive in going to Canterbury 'with ful devout corage'. Chaucer plays upon this duality between religious and sensual motives throughout the complex portraits that follow.

Second, the pilgrims themselves form a provocative cross-section of society and are placed in an original situation. There are the Knight and his son, the Squire, from the gentry. Their servant is a yeoman. The Church is represented by the Prioresse, who travels with another nun and three priests, the Monk, the Friar, the Parson, and two non-clerical Church employees engaged in corrupt Church business: the Summoner who works for an ecclesiastical court, and the Pardoner who sells indulgences. There are the town guildsmen with their cook, and a representative sample of various trades and professions ranging from the lowly Plowman, the Miller, the Reeve and the Manciple, to the Sergeant at Lawe, the Physician, the Shipman and the Merchant. Finally there are the Wife of Bath, the Franklin, the learned Clerk and Chaucer himself. The group of pilgrims contains representatives from all the major branches of society, both secular and clerical, 'gentil' and common, rural and urban. Once they accept the Host's offer, however, Chaucer's most original achievement becomes apparent: the thirty pilgrims form a varied but almost classless society. Feudal and economic distinctions disappear as they all bow to the authority of Harry Bailey, the common man. Chaucer's artificial society of equals is a very modern group in the sense already explained: the Host is typical of the new urban classes, a man of little education and no birth, but with good business sense, sound common sense and some social position. The real Harry Bailey served in several local offices and sat for Southwark in the Parliaments of 1376–7 and 1378–9. The pilgrims, then, are under the authority of a modern man.

We will meet and refer to some of the pilgrims in the general commentary. However, it is always helpful to keep in mind the extraordinary audience the Wife of Bath spoke to: a representative cross-section of fourteenth-century society that she handles with the skill of a great comic.

2.2 THE WIFE'S PLACE AMONG THE PILGRIMS

The Wife's portrait is one of the most pregnant in 'The General Prologue', containing a number of hints that are resolved or expanded later when she speaks for herself. Chaucer says that she 'was somdel deef', a reference to the incident she recounts in her Prologue when her fifth husband hit her on the ear. Her travels to the shrines of Europe are also mentioned – she had been to Jerusalem three times, to Rome and Boulogne, Compostella and Cologne. When she later tells the story of her life she hints that most of these journeys took place during her fourth and least satisfactory marriage. Finally, her promiscuity is mentioned coyly. She had five husbands:

Withouten oother compaignye in youthe, –
But therof nedeth nat to speke as nowthe. (Robinson, p.21)

Chaucer's shy self-consciousness here sets the scene for comic use of ambiguity to hint at the Wife's sexual adventures, a tone of innuendo that she uses outrageously in her own Prologue. Chaucer remarks with apparent innocence that 'She was a worthy womman al hir lyve', allowing 'worthy' to change its meaning as he explains that she has survived a lot of men. His comment on her travels is that 'She koude muchel of wandrynge by the weye', with the implication that she did not keep to the path of righteousness, but played among the sinful by-ways during her travels. This is reinforced by explicit reference to her lechery in 'Gat-tothed was she'. Finally, she was an expert in 'remedies of love'. The phrase means cures for love, but in her own Prologue Alison assumes that the only cure for sexual desire is sexual satisfaction, so the compliment to her sexual ability is clearly intended and underlined by the final line, 'For she koude of that art the olde daunce'.

Her personality is vividly portrayed. She is vain of her social position and quick-tempered if anyone tries to take precedence over her. Chaucer makes this point more telling by using the example of the collection in Church and remarking that her anger puts her 'out of alle charitee'. Temporal things are clearly more important to Alison than her religion. She is an extrovert, wearing scarlet stockings and having a 'boold' face and 'hipes large'. She is an aggressive, dominating personality who rides 'esily', wears 'a paire of spores sharpe' and a hat that is likened to 'a bokeler or a targe'. Finally, she is lively and sociable, able to 'laughe and carpe', giving a forceful impression of her confidence and ability to trade jokes with the varied and mostly male pilgrims. Her ability to handle coarse men is shown later, when first the Pardoner, then the Summoner and the Friar, interrupt her.

In the group as a whole, Alison stands out in two respects. First, she belongs with the moderns: she is well-off, one of the new middle class of self-made people; her pride and jealousy of trivial social position compares with the vanity of the guildsmen's wives who are ambitious to be called 'madame'. She would belong nowhere or anywhere in the old feudal order, but has the energy and earthy common sense of the new who make and take a social position for themselves. In this respect she belongs in a group with the guildsmen, the Franklin and the Host himself; and she contrasts with the unworldly learning and orthodoxy of, say, the Clerk.

Secondly, she takes a significant place in the duality between the religious and the sensual. In *The General Prologue* we can see two distinct positive qualities set against all the hypocrisy and greed Chaucer reveals. The first of these is the honest goodness embodied in the Parson as a spiritual pastor, his unselfish brother the Plowman, and found to a lesser extent in the stern self-discipline of the Knight. The second quality is vitality, an indulgent and sensual enjoyment of life, which is portrayed as an attractive attribute. The pilgrims who possess this quality are sinful, but they are warm, frank and exciting. Alison is clearly placed as the most vivid of these, comparable to the Monk and to some extent the Franklin. This is a group of people we are inclined to like in spite of their obvious faults.

The Wife of Bath occupies a focal position among the pilgrims, then. Not only is she in stark contrast to moral goodness and religious truth (she is as sinful as they come!); her openness and honesty also put her in contrast to the many hypocrisies of the pilgrims, from the Summoner's vulgar falsehoods to the subtle and dishonest cloak of courtly manners that covers the Squire's passion.

2.3 THE MARRIAGE GROUP OF TALES

Chaucer develops *The Canterbury Tales* in a complex way. They are entertaining stories, but each Tale also suits and reveals the character of the pilgrim telling it, and contributes to the development of themes that run through the work as a whole. This integration of characters and themes within a developing context makes many people see *The Canterbury Tales* as the forerunner of the great novels of English literature. This section will look briefly at the main issues raised in 'The Wife of Bath's Prologue and Tale', and will sketch their development in other tales.

Alison of Bath announces her theme in her first three lines. She has enough experience to 'speke of wo that is in mariage'. She argues that women should have 'soveraynetee' and dominate their husbands. Women will win 'soveraynetee' by cultivating a combative attitude she calls 'maistrye'. Her Tale adds complexity to the theme of marriage by introducing the idea of 'gentillesse' – noble and virtuous behaviour – in contrast to 'maistrye'. The Wife's provocative assertion inspires fierce reactions and debate among the pilgrims. Several later tales contribute to the theme, but this section looks at 'gentillesse', 'maistrye' and the theme of marriage through 'The Clerk's Tale', 'The Merchant's Tale' and 'The Franklin's Tale'.

The Clerk's Tale

The Wife of Bath argued that women must intimidate and rule their husbands to gain 'soveraynetee' in marriage. The Clerk's Tale of patient Griselda takes up Alison's militant challenge. His Tale is of a marriage in which the husband, Walter, tests his wife Griselda for humility and obedience over a period of thirteen years. First he appears to have their children taken away and murdered, then he pretends to divorce her and keep her as a servant while he marries a young girl. Unknown to Griselda the young bride is actually their thirteen-year-old daughter who has been secretly brought up elsewhere. When Walter sees that his wife is obedient even under this treatment, he reveals the deception and praises her patience. Throughout the Tale Griselda's patience is extolled, and her submission to Walter's 'maistrye' is praised. On the surface, this would seem to be a tale to redress the balance: it asserts the man's absolute authority in marriage, and praises the virtues of 'pacience' and obedience that the Wife of Bath so obviously lacks.

The Clerk's Tale is ironic, however, and cannot be read as a flat contradiction of the Wife. First, the Clerk does not recommend Griselda's patience as a pattern for other women:

> This storie is seyd, nat for that wyves sholde
> Folwen Grisilde as in humylitee,
> For it were inportable, though they wolde. (Robinson, p. 113)

He recognises that real women would not submit to suffering as patiently as the miraculous Griselda. He then ironically recommends the opposite, urging women to be dominating and aggressive. The song with which he ends his Tale is heavily tongue-in-cheek and the audience recognises his caricature of the Wife of Bath:

> Ye archewyves, stondeth at defense,
> Syn ye be strong as is a greet camaille. . .
> . . .Beth egre as is a tygre yond in Ynde;
> Ay clappeth as a mille, I yow consaille. (Robinson, p. 114)

Just as Griselda's patience is beyond possibility, so Walter's 'maistrye' is too extreme. Several critics have thought that Walter is a sadist. The Clerk emphasises that he had an irrational compulsion to torture his wife, and criticises him for this:

> But wedded men ne knowe no mesure,
> Whan that they fynde a pacient creature. (Robinson, p. 108)

Walter's 'maistrye', then, is a sickness of mind leading to cruel excess; the Wife's 'maistrye' is satirically caricatured in the picture of an 'arch-wife' like a camel or a tiger. The Clerk is not attacking women at all: he is attacking 'maistrye' itself, the aggressive cruelty that kills happiness and causes suffering.

In addition, the Clerk supports the Wife's ideas about 'gentillesse'. She argued that nobility of character comes from God, and can be found in all ranks of society: it is not inherited from 'noble' ancestors. The Clerk, whose sadistic Walter is an aristocrat and who extols perfect patience in the lowly-born Griselda, fully endorses this modern, egalitarian view:

> For God it woot, that children ofte been
> Unlyk hir worthy eldres hem bifore;
> Bountee comth al of God, nat of the streen
> Of which they been engendred and ybore. (Robinson, p. 102)

Finally, the Clerk widens the debate by recommending patience not because we ought to submit to sadists like Walter, but because our trials are sent by God who 'preeveth folk al day'. It is God who allows us to be 'bete in sondry wise' with 'sharpe scourges of adversitee', and we should suffer in 'pacience' for the sake of our eternal salvation.

The Merchant's Tale

'The Merchant's Tale' tells of an old man, Januarye, who marries a young wife, May. She has an affair with his squire, Damyan. Januarye sees them but May answers his accusation so cunningly that he is duped. This tale has little to say about 'maistrye' and 'gentillesse'. Instead, the Merchant returns to the battle of the sexes, and the problem of marriages between old and young, raised by the Wife of Bath. He underlines the inappropriateness of marriage between 'tendre youthe' and 'stoupynge age', and makes a lot of fun of old Januarye's attempts to satisfy young May's desires. The main point that emerges, however, is that 'carnal' desire is an evil guide, and appears in many deceptive guises. Januarye pretends that his lust is not a sin because they are married:

> And blessed be the yok that we been inne,
> For in oure actes we mowe do no synne. (Robinson, p. 121)

The Merchant makes it clear elsewhere that sexual desire is a sin whether in or out of wedlock, so Januarye's statement is a delusion, a cloak for his lechery.

Damyan, the squire, adopts 'courtly love' manners to dissemble his lust. It is clear, however, that he suffers from physical desire and nothing else, as it is said that he 'dyeth for desyr'. In Damyan, the idea that love inspires goodness is cynically mocked: his illicit lust inspires hypocrisy and fraud. Damyan made himself pleasant to all, particularly the old husband he was betraying:

> And eek to Januarie he gooth as lowe
> As evere dide a dogge for the bowe. (Robinson, p. 122)

The lust of the young wife May is easily seen when she climbs so nimbly up the pear tree where Damyan awaits her. But even she deceives herself in a mockery of 'courtly' ideals, saying lustfully that 'pitee renneth soone in gentil herte'.

In this tale of cynical humour, deception, lechery and cunning, the Merchant points out the many deceptive disguises that cover lust, and exhorts us to shun sexual desires for our own safety:

> O perilous fyr, that in the bedstraw bredeth!
> O famulier foo, that his servyce bedeth! (Robinson, p. 120)

The Franklin's Tale

'The Franklin's Tale' is the most subtle and ironic of the 'marriage' group of tales. Briefly, the marriage between Arveragus and Dorigen is the result of a 'courtly' courtship, and when they marry each vows submission to the other, so it is seemingly a marriage with no 'maistrye' on either side. When Arveragus is away, Dorigen despairs and a squire called Aurelius declares his love for her. She rejects him, but because her mind is dominated by an obsessive fantasy that her returning husband's ship will be wrecked, she promises to be his love if he can make all the rocks disappear from around the coast. Aurelius then nearly dies from despair, but two years later pays a magician to remove the rocks from the coast. He then goes to claim Dorigen's love. Arveragus has returned in the meantime, and Dorigen asks him what she should do. He puts 'trouthe' to her promise above everything else and sends her to Aurelius. This selfless act, and pity for Dorigen's misery, inspire Aurelius to send her back again; and when he tells the magician how nobly Arveragus and he have both acted, this inspires the magician to let him off paying for the spell, which should have cost his whole fortune.

The Franklin's treatment of his Tale is subtle and ambiguous. In terms of the themes we are interested in, however, the following points stand out. First, he agrees with the Wife and the Clerk that 'gentillesse' is not hereditary. The magician points out that all classes are equally capable of gentillesse:

> Thou art a squier, and he is a knyght;
> But God forbede, for his blisful myght,
> But if a clerk koude doon a gentil dede
> As wel as any of yow, it is no drede! (Robinson, p. 144)

Secondly, the Franklin agrees with the Clerk that 'maistrye' is destructive:

> Love wol nat been constreyned by maistrye.
> Whan maistrie comth, the God of love anon
> Beteth his wynges, and farewel, he is gon! (Robinson, p. 136)

He also agrees that the most important virtue in marriage is 'pacience', borrowing a term from the Clerk, but links this with 'gentillesse' redefined in terms of 'temperaunce' and forgiveness. The real evil in 'The Franklin's Tale' seems to be any single-minded obsession: Aurelius's passion is excessive, and blinds him to the sinfulness of seduction and adultery; Arveragus's devotion to 'trouthe' and honour is excessive, and leads him into the moral absurdity of commanding his wife to commit adultery. Finally, Dorigen's obsessive fear of the rocks is excessive and leads her to give a false promise to Aurelius. People's obsessions lead them to make mistakes, and the way to preserve happiness is through unselfish and forgiving, or 'gentil', deeds, like the three actions of Arveragus, Aurelius and the Clerk that bring about the happy ending to this tale.

The Franklin's encomium on 'pacience' deserves to be quoted in full, for it shows how far Chaucer's pilgrims have collectively added depth and subtlety to the themes so stridently announced by the Wife of Bath:

> Pacience is an heigh vertu, certeyn,
> For it venquysseth, as thise clerkes seyn,
> Thynges that rigour sholde nevere atteyne.
> For every word men may nat chide or pleyne.
> Lerneth to suffre, or elles, so moot I goon,
> Ye shul it lerne, wher so ye wole or noon;
> For in this world, certein, ther no wight is
> That he ne dooth or seith somtyme amys.
> Ire, siknesse, or constellacioun,
> Wyn, wo, or chaungynge of complexioun
> Causeth ful ofte to doon amys or speken.
> On every wrong a man may nat be wreken. (Robinson, p. 136)

The Franklin's recommendation of 'gentillesse' also rests on the idea that one 'gentil' act will inspire others, so people will inspire each other and goodness will spread. This is a far cry from the Wife of Bath's cynical view that marriage is a battle without mercy: any sign of forgiveness would seem like fatal weakness in her eyes.

If you are studying 'The Wife of Bath's Prologue and Tale', it is worth your while to read the other tales discussed here. It is best to read them in the original, of course, but you may find Nevill Coghill's modern version quicker to read and easier to approach, in the Penguin edition of *The Canterbury Tales*.

3 THE LITERARY

BACKGROUND

3.1 'THE WIFE OF BATH'S PROLOGUE AND TALE': RHETORIC, LEARNING AND COMIC REALISM

This section gives a brief account of the main sources Chaucer drew upon, and the Wife of Bath's style in relation to medieval literary conventions, leaving more detailed explanations of her many references for the general commentary.

Rhetoric

'Rhetoric' is a word used loosely nowadays to denote any overdone or insincere style. In medieval times it was an exact term for a respected science: the science of speaking and writing in the most persuasive and harmonious manner. A 'rhetorical' argument would be carefully supported with references to the Bible and other 'auctoritees'; it would follow logical rules of construction, each section would be composed to a particular tone or 'colour', and the writer or speaker would take care to ensure smooth transitions between the different sections. The aim of the science of 'rhetoric' was to ensure that speeches and writings were orderly, based on secure wisdom, and gave pleasure to the audience by being elegantly expressed. The Wife of Bath's first line announces that she will not argue her case according to the rules of rhetoric, because she is speaking from 'experience' and 'noon auctoritee'. However, to say that she does not use rhetoric would be too simple, for she is familiar with some of its techniques and uses them on occasion.

Alison of Bath is a consummate public speaker. When she announces her theme at the beginning of her Prologue, she first quotes the main arguments against 'bigamye', referring to Christ's words to the Samaritan woman; by line 35 she is citing other 'auctoritees' to support her case, showing familiarity with Solomon and St Paul and using some standard rhetorical techniques, such as the series of persuasive questions about the purpose of genitals that leads to a typically balanced and 'rhetorical' conclusion:

> Why sholde men elles in hir bookes sette
> That man shal yelde to his wyf hire dette?
> Now wherwith sholde he make his paiement,
> If he ne used his sely instrument?
> Thanne were they maad upon a creature
> To purge uryne, and eek for engendrure. (lines 129–34)

Later in the Prologue we are again aware of her knowledge of rhetoric. Jankyn, her learned fifth husband, used to rail at her using example after example of wicked women from the past. We notice the way his speech builds to a climax by quoting five proverbs in the space of ten lines (lines 775–85). Alison knows something of rhetoric, then, but there is no sustained rhetorical passage until the old wife in her tale speaks about 'gentillesse'. Generally, Alison uses rhetorical techniques intermittently, and then largely so that she can abuse them by stretching logic or suddenly changing tone and subject. In conclusion, then, Chaucer presents her as a character with some knowledge of medieval conventions of oratory; but the main interest of her style lies in how her natural volatility and outrageous views distort and break the conventions of medieval order.

Learning

The same point is borne out when we study her learning. 'The Wife of Bath's Prologue and Tale' is studded with references to texts that she no doubt met during her marriage to Jankyn the clerk. In particular, Jankyn had a book of 'wikked wyves' which was a compilation of anti-feminist stories and tracts. He used this as 'auctoritee' in his constant abuse of Alison. We can guess how bitterly she came to know these references and stories; but in her Prologue she not only gives a long example of Jankyn reading from his book, but also frequently refers to the same authors in her own discourse. Her opening arguments about bigamy and chastity, for example, draw heavily on her knowledge of St Jerome's *Epistle Against Jovinian*, and elsewhere she makes numerous references to the Roman historian Valerius Maximus. The detailed knowledge of St Paul's first Epistle to the Corinthians that she shows at the beginning of her

Prologue could also have come from Jerome's work, for he quotes this source at length.

The fact that Alison's learning has all been gained at second hand is emphasised in her Tale when she relates the story of Midas, saying that his wife betrayed the secret of his ass's ears. The original story appears in Ovid's *Metamorphoses* where Midas's barber betrays him, not his wife. The mistake was probably a deliberate change Jankyn had made to suit his anti-feminist purpose, and Alison mis-reports the story quite innocently.

However, the overriding impression we gain from looking at the 'auctoritees' used in Alison's narrative, is that she refers to them in order to distort them. Several examples of this will be discussed in the general commentary section. One typical instance is the connection she draws between a remark from Paul's Epistle to Timothy, that a lord has both gold and wooden vessels in his household, and another reference to Paul's Epistle to the Corinthians where the Apostle points out that different people are called to God for their different gifts. By thoroughly distorting both authorities, the Wife manages to claim that her sexual appetite is a divine 'yifte' and that God has called her to be promiscuous! The Wife of Bath's learning, then, becomes a measure of her unconventionality, showing us clearly how far she mistakes and distorts the moral and spiritual wisdom of her time. D. W. Robertson, in his *A Preface to Chaucer*, analyses Alison's misuse of 'auctoritees' in detail (see Further Reading).

Comic realism

The Wife of Bath would initially strike Chaucer's audience as a fairly conventional comic figure. Such figures from the lower strata of society were quite common in medieval literature, and would frequently come forward frankly and shockingly to confess their sinfulness. Alison, with her outrageous immorality, sharp spurs and scarlet stockings, is at first a comic figure of this kind, and might belong in an allegorical play representing a particular sin such as lechery. Chaucer goes far beyond the tradition, however, and there is no source or precedent for her development as a complex character in the modern sense of the word. She has personal experiences and emotions, a convincingly real and individual personality, and not only deals with a confession of her cardinal sins but also discusses more serious and wide-ranging concerns. In the comic tradition of the time, characterisation was generally limited to portraying a particular sin, while philosophical discussions were carried on between nobler characters, the knights and gentlefolk. In this sense Alison is an entirely original creation; and in the development of English literature she stands as the founder of a later tradition, giving rise to great and complex comic characters such as Shakespeare's Shylock and Falstaff.

3.2 'THE WIFE OF BATH'S TALE': SOURCES

Alison's tale is of a young knight sentenced to death for rape, who has to answer a question to save his life. The figure of the old hag who gives him the answer and whom he is consequently forced to marry, and the magical ending after he submits to her 'soveraynetee', make the choice of tale suitable to the character of Alison as revealed in her Prologue. There are a number of similar stories Chaucer may have drawn upon, the most notable of which are Gower's tale of *Florent* and the contemporary romance, *The Wedding of Sir Gawayn and Dame Ragnell*. The similarities between these and Chaucer's story are many, but there are also several differences and most scholars think it likely that the stories were written independently. They are all, however, based on a common folklore story that appears in popular ballads of the time also, so there is no need to establish a single direct source for Chaucer's version. The old wife or 'loathly lady', the life-question, the choice between beauty and ugliness, and the knight's submission that lifts the enchantment she is under: all these elements have many precedents and analogues and Chaucer makes a fairly clear adaptation of them to suit his own – and Alison of Bath's – purposes.

Although there is probably no direct source for the whole tale, it is worth noticing that Chaucer incorporates some features directly drawn from his reading and his own earlier writings. In this connection we should notice that the old wife's character, like that of Alison herself, shows some indebtedness to the figure of La Vieille from *Romaunt of the Rose*, Chaucer's translation from Jean de Meun; and that the centrepiece of her long speech, the lecture on the subject of 'gentillesse', is a compilation of examples and ideas brought together from Chaucer's translation *Romaunt of the Rose*, his 'Ballade of Gentillesse', Dante's *Convivio* (which Chaucer undoubtedly knew), and Boethius, the philosopher Chaucer translated into English as *Boece*.

3.3 CHAUCER'S TREATMENT

From this account we can see that Chaucer drew on a wide variety of sources, and was prepared to use any suitable material that came to hand in order to create the Wife and her Tale. As with any artist, however, it is not so much what raw stuff he happens to use as what he does with it that is original or significant. Alison is an utterly original creation far outstripping any of the sources used in her Prologue or her Tale: she is much more complex and fascinating than the allegorical figures that may have suggested her to Chaucer, or even La Vieille from the *Romaunt*. The main interest in looking at Chaucer's sources lies in how they relate to an overall duality between medieval and modern views.

The Wife of Bath seems to use rhetoric and learning largely so that she can distort or abuse them. 'Rhetoric' imposed an orderly system of rules on to speech and writing, and learning was the natural buttress for medieval authority and order. These prescribed and solemn systems belong to the older view of the world that I have called medieval. Chaucer uses them as part of his portrayal of a changing world: the self-centred energy and self-confidence of a new outlook was shaking the old edifices of feudal society and the established Church. So the Wife of Bath, undoubtedly a modern person and showing scant respect for conventions of any kind, mangles, twists and kicks around the tatters of 'auctoritee' which have come her way. At the same time Chaucer uses her learning ironically to reveal her limitations. 'Auctoritee' was a subtle and moral system of thought. The modern Wife can make it appear ridiculous, but she does not properly understand it. Part of Chaucer's triumph lies in the way he creates the duality of the fourteenth-century world, portraying it as an ambiguous skirmish between Alison of Bath and her much abused 'auctoritees'.

4 THE COMMENTARY

The wife argues her case (lines 1–162)

The opening of the Wife's Prologue gives us an immediate sense of her personality. The style is dramatic, impressing the Wife's distinctive voice on the reader and using variations of pace and tone to create pauses or changes in volume so that we can hear how she manipulates her audience. The opening part is also appropriate to her character. Her portrait in *The General Prologue* mentions her spurs and shield-like hat, so we are ready to meet a combative personality. It is no surprise, therefore, that her first aim when she speaks is to defend herself and to attack her critics.

The Wife sets out to counter two arguments which have been brought against 'bigamye', by which she means both marrying more than once in a lifetime, as in her own case, and having more than one spouse simultaneously, as in the legal sense. These two arguments take their origins from the Bible. First, Alison mentions Christ's words to the Samaritan woman from John, 4, where He said that the woman had five husbands, and 'that ilke man that now hath thee is noght thyn housbonde'. The substance of this argument against bigamy is that Christ disapproved of people who marry too often. Secondly, Alison refers to the discussion of chastity, marriage, separation and remarriage from St Paul's 'First Epistle to the Corinthians', taking several of the Apostle's points in some detail. Paul recommends chastity but does not command it; and he recommends that a widow should not marry again, but does not command this either, saying that she is free to marry again should she choose to.

The Wife of Bath finds a variety of answers to these authorities, but her strength does not lie in any serious attempt to win a theological debate. Rather, she uses the debate to launch her own shameless assertion of vitality. She begins by pressing two of St Paul's ideas into service to support her, then develops them to a point of scurrilous absurdity that Paul would never have dreamed of. We can see how Alison turns biblical ammunition to her own purpose by examining what happens to Paul's ideas in her hands.

The Wife correctly reports the Apostle's words 'Bet is to be wedded than to brynne'. However, as she has just declared that she will never be 'chaast in al' and is busy searching for a sixth husband, the word 'brynne' has a delicious ambiguity: does it mean to burn in Hell from the sin of intercourse, or to burn with frustrated sexual desire? This innuendo is developed later when she uses the image of fire for sexual desire and fulfilment – 'peril is both fyr and tow t'assemble'. As these double meanings develop, St Paul's original concern with sin and virtue is overlaid by a strong new impression which comes from the Wife herself. Her innuendo and imagery suggest that chastity is unnatural: people must have intercourse regularly, runs the argument, so it will be less sinful if they are married.

Other elements are woven into Alison's discourse, increasing the sense of urgent desire. For example, she insists that our genitals were given us for 'ese of engendrure' as well as to help us excrete; and develops this idea to the point where it seems irreligious to refuse intercourse: 'I wol use myn instrument as frely as my Makere hath it sent. If I be daungerous, God yeve me sorwe!' Her technique, then, is to take what appears to be a reasonable argument, then draw it into her network of sexual innuendo and imagery until it becomes outrageously distorted.

The second point Alison borrows from St Paul is that chastity is not commanded, only recommended. Again her starting point is a correct reference: 'al nys but conseil to virginitee'; but she links this 'indulgence' with the idea that different people are called to God in different ways, so each of us is favoured with a different 'yifte' from God. Alison is satisfied to be ordinary and does not attempt the higher perfection of 'maydenhede'. She is like a wooden vessel in God's house, valueless compared to a chaste saint – a vessel of gold – but equally useful. She describes the chaste as 'pured whete-seed' while wives are 'barly-breed'. These images are drawn out of context from Chapter 2 of the Second Epistle to Timothy. Alison does not mention that wooden vessels tend 'to dishonour', and as she changes the context, St Paul's meaning is distorted. She says she has been called by God for her special gift of sexuality:

> In swich estaat as God hath cleped us
> I wol persevere; I nam nat precius.

She then refers to Christ using 'barly-breed' in the miracle of the loaves, when he 'refresshed many a man'. The common contemporary innuendo on 'refreshment' for sexual satisfaction gives a picture of Alison satisfying five thousand men, and scurrilously suggests that she and her unlimited sexual appetite are a miracle created by Christ.

Alison adds further arguments in favour of marriage, borrowing from her knowledge of St Jerome and citing biblical examples of 'bigamye' from Abraham and Jacob to Solomon. There is further humour in these examples, for they are of men who had many spouses at once, not as in Alison's case one at a time, and she makes comic play of Solomon by complimenting his sexual stamina and wishing she could 'be refresshed half so ofte as he!'. Finally, we should notice that she uses St Paul's assertion that wives own their husbands' bodies; and that she introduces a commercial image for intercourse in the idea – also drawn from Paul – that husbands should pay their 'dette' to their wives. These two strands of thought are announced here in Alison's opening debate, but will undergo important developments in the remainder of the text.

The main point we notice at the beginning of the Wife's Prologue, then, is her ability to create outrageous double meanings and develop comic effects by pushing the advice of 'auctoritee' to an absurd conclusion. At the same time, Chaucer announces themes and images that will be used both by Alison herself to advance her central assertion of a woman's right to 'soveraynetee' in marriage; and ironically by Chaucer for the dramatic purpose of revealing inner aspects of Alison's character. Thus the wide variety of ideas, brought together so shockingly in this opening section, form a basis we will refer to repeatedly as we examine the rest of the text.

Chaucer, then, has created a powerful personality who turns what purports to be a debate into an attack on established values, an assertion that sexual activity is good, natural and blessed by God. This unconventional thought is complemented by the vivid voice of the Wife of Bath, which is created largely through Chaucer's masterful use of rhythm and pace, and sudden contrasts in diction.

The pace of Alison's speech varies sharply, between a helter-skelter rush, such as the answer she gives to her own rhetorical questions:

> Yet herde I nevere tellen in my age
> Upon this nombre diffinicioun.

and a slower, more broken rhythm with frequent interjections and parentheses, that seems to ramble and often precedes the rapid punch-line of her next joke. A good example of this occurs when she is preparing her audience for a joke about Solomon's wondrous stamina:

> God woot, this noble kyng, as to my wit,
> The firste nyght had many a myrie fit
> With ech of hem. . .

The first of these lines is broken into three phrases, two of which ('God woot' and 'as to my wit') are mere filling-in; but the scandalous joke comes out in a rush in the next line.

Frequent use of parentheses also helps create the impression that she is thinking as she speaks, an impression enhanced by her habit of asking rhetorical questions and then adding supplementary questions that express the same idea in different words, as she does in line 23. All these techniques help in bringing her to life as a dramatic figure.

Alison's diction is full of sudden changes and contrasts: it is an idiosyncratic mixture. We can identify three distinct tones in the opening section, beginning with the argumentative diction she employs in lines 10–13, with its bookish phrases such as 'that by the same ensample taughte he me', and a sentence construction exhibiting the balance of scholastic argument. Interspersed among these demonstrations of learning we find colloquialisms such as 'for the nones' or the repeated 'Lo!' to call her audience's attention. Some colloquial words appear in a context of literary diction, as 'sely' in line 132 applies to the euphemism 'instrument' and closely follows 'office' and 'engendrure'; and in these cases there is a deliberate bathetic effect. Finally, Alison has masterly command of arch *double-entendre*, using 'refresshed', 'pay his dette', 'bothe thynges smale', 'brynne', 'instrument' and 'harneys' among many other words and phrases that fill her speech with more or less open references to sexuality.

The Pardoner's interruption (lines 163–92)

Alison is exulting in her 'power' over her husband's body when the Pardoner interrupts. Some background knowledge of the Pardoner will show the absurdity of what he says. He is described in 'The General Prologue' as 'a geldyng or a mare'; in other words, he has either been castrated or his sexual organs have never developed. He has a high squeaky voice, no beard, and long yellow hair. At the end of the 'Pardoner's Tale' the Host insults him with a reference to his lack of testicles, so the Pardoner's impotence is clearly evident to all pilgrims.

In this context his claim that he was about to marry but will now cancel his wedding because he does not want his body destroyed by too much sexual activity, is ridiculous. All the pilgrims understand the joke: he is only using the Wife's outspoken aggression as an excuse for not being married. Alison's reply is typically combative, calling the Pardoner's bluff. Listening to her is like drinking strong ale, and she promises to open another barrel that will taste more bitter than the one already broached. The strong drink she will offer is her experience of marriage, and when she has finished she will give him a chance to taste it. By implication she is saying that he should listen carefully, then decide whether he wants to be her sixth husband. She warns him that the sixth husband will suffer: her taste will be 'wors than ale' and in marriage she has been the 'whippe'. She also warns him to be careful what he says to her, because she is armed with enough learned examples from 'auctoritee' to outdo him in debate as well.

The Pardoner has had too much to drink and finds he is out of his depth. He extricates himself from embarrassment by begging her to proceed: but there are two stings even in his conciliatory words. First he repeats his absurd boast, claiming to be a 'yonge' man eager to learn what Alison can teach about marriage and sex. Secondly, his words imply that she is old, and thus attack her on a vulnerable front, as we will discover later. Alison replies in a soothing manner also, and begs the Pardoner and the rest of her audience not to take offence at what she says: the purpose of her 'Prologue and Tale' is 'nat but for to pleye'. She expects that she will be taken lightly, then, not wishing to give offence. We will be able to assess how honestly she means this, and how far it comes true, when we look at the text as a whole. There is obvious irony, however, for she is deliberately shocking, and her theme of marriage becomes a serious debate through the medium of other pilgrims and their tales (see Chapter 2 above).

The first three husbands (lines 193–451)

Alison proceeds with the story of her own life by giving an account of her first three marriages. She does not specify her age or the number of years each marriage lasted, and does not differentiate between the three men she was married to: instead, she portrays her first three

husbands as a single composite figure and builds up a picture of her
life with them by describing their relationship in general terms and
giving an example of how she spoke to them, in the form of a long
monologue in direct speech. In this part of her narrative Alison
develops ideas on love and the battle of the sexes, while at the same
time Chaucer subtly reveals further ironical insights into her
character.

Alison begins by asserting a shockingly cynical view: that her first
three husbands were 'goode' being 'riche, and olde'. This announces
the inversion of conventional morality she elaborates throughout the
rest of her Prologue. The word 'goode' is stripped of its usual
connotations by the context: perhaps we expect a 'goode' husband to
be handsome, loving and strong, bringing happiness to his wife; but
the words 'riche, and olde' give the actual sense in which she
describes them as good: they are submissive, weak and ill, soon dead,
easy to fool and quickly parted from their money and lands. This
anti-idealism and degradation of love and marriage to the cynical
values of power and money occurs repeatedly and is emphasised by
the recurrent images she chooses. Her descriptions of marriage thus
build up a cynical philosophy of 'love' that has no room for
sentiment. It is an inversion of common morality that treats avarice
and pride as laudable virtues. Obviously Alison is aware of the comic
potential in her shocking views; and there is a sense in which she is
merely being honest about society's attitudes to marriage. However,
it would be premature to assess how far she is conscious of irony, and
how far Chaucer uses it to reveal her character, at this stage. Full
discussion of this vexed question will have to wait until after the
commentary.

Alison's imagery in this part of the Prologue adds to the degradation of love and marriage. She uses three kinds of image to denote
love, husbands, wives and the marital relationship. First she compares people to a number of commodities and possessions of a
common kind, continuing the strand of imagery she began when she
claimed to be a wooden vessel in God's household. In this section,
wives are compared to a 'spaynel' bitch leaping on a dog, a 'grey
goose', then 'oxen, asses, hors and houndes', 'bacyns, lavours',
'spoones and stooles', 'pottes, clothes, and array', and a cat. She
claims that she could 'byte and whyne' like a horse, compares herself
to a hawk and her husband's body to old meat – 'bacon' – while he is
a mad lion, who should be like a sheep. The effect of these
comparisons is to create a world in which there are only common,
everyday utensils and animals, and this gives a tone of vulgarity to the
whole passage.

Second, the absolute power of sexual desire is emphasised again by use of the fire imagery we met in her opening sallies. First Alison's sex is the flame of her husband's candle that cannot be confined but, in the nature of flames, will light other candles; then women's love is likened to 'wilde fyr' that:

> The moore it brenneth, the moore it hath desir
> To consume every thyng that brent wole be.

The two aspects of fire that are brought out are its freedom to spread and its destructive power, so women's promiscuity and their ability to consume men with their sexual demands are highlighted.

Finally Alison compares love and marriage with commerce. We met this strand of thought in the first section when she compared a husband's lovemaking with paying a debt to his wife; but the intermingling of commercial terms with bribes and ransomes in Alison's account of her first three husbands develops the view that a woman's sexual favours have a price, and their commercial value increases when she denies gratification. She tells her husbands that they would like to lock her in their chest, with their valuables; and she links desire with profit saying that she no longer values a man who has given her all his property:

> What sholde I taken keep hem for to plese,
> But it were for my profit and myn ese?

Later she explains how she gained all her husbands' wealth by demanding payment for her favours: 'I wolde no lenger in the bed abyde . . . til he had maad his raunson unto me'. The parallel with prostitution is obvious, so the link between love and commerce serves to further vulgarise love and marriage.

The picture Alison builds, then, is shockingly cynical. Two further points complete the degradation of marriage. First, the bulk of this passage consists of a monologue in which Alison supposedly tells her husband what he said to her when he was drunk, and this turns out to be a long tirade against women. Although these are supposedly an imaginary man's words, we should also remember that Alison invents this long male chauvinist diatribe herself. How far the sustained misogyny of this speech represents Alison's own feelings is a question for later, but it is worth noting that her direct statements to the audience of pilgrims also show a degrading view of women, echoing the opinions she puts into her husbands' mouths. Alison says that 'Deceite, wepyng, spynnyng God hath yive to wommen kyndely', and claims that these dishonest forms of 'wit' are given to women 'in oure birthe'.

Second, Alison leaves no room for equality between husband and wife. In her opinion, marriage is a battle for supremacy and there can be no compromise. She makes this quite clear, explaining that her motive for marrying was solely 'for my profit and myn ese', and insisting that the main point of which she is proud is her victory over these three husbands:

> . . . of o thyng I avaunte me,
> Atte ende I hadde the bettre in ech degree.

Finally she insists that one or other partner in marriage must be in charge: 'Oon of us two moste bowen, doutelees'. In the whole of the passage, then, Alison takes the attitude that sexual desire is abolutely powerful, dominating everyone; that the attraction of anything increases when it is rare or unattainable, and conversely that nothing you already have is desirable; and that men and women fight for victory over each other in their marriages without compromise or mercy.

Altogether she gives a damning indictment of human nature. There are, however, some subtle aspects of her management of the first three husbands, and we should notice how cleverly she manipulates their weaknesses to enhance her power. She flatters them by pretending jealousy as if they might be unfaithful to her. These old husbands were worn out by her sexual demands, so sick they could barely stand, yet she says:

> Yet tikled I his herte, for that he
> Wened that I hadde of hym so greet chiertee!

She also agrees with their misogyny to gain power, pointing out that men are 'moore resonable', so they should give in when there are arguments. Alison does feign affection for her husbands. Although she finds them repulsive she admits she is willing to 'make me a feyned appetit' when they have paid for her favours; and we hear an affectionate tone of voice as she speaks to them rather as if they were children: 'com neer, my spouse, lat me ba thy cheke!' In these ways, then, she panders to their pride even while taking advantage of their weaknesses as 'olde' men.

There is a constant counter-current added to this vein of flattery, for Alison reminds them of their insecurity at the same time. When she offers to be faithful to them, for example, she says 'Wy, taak it al! lo, have it every deel!', but immediately reminds them how much she could earn if she chose to sell her sex to others. Again, when she protests the purity of her relations with Jankyn the page, declaring that she would not sleep with him if her husband died tomorrow, she couples this loyal promise with a description of the page dwelling on his fresh, youthful attractions in contrast to the husband's age. She manipulates the first three husbands cleverly indeed.

This part of the narrative also contains the first signs of an ironic counter-truth that contradicts and complicates our initial image of the Wife's character. The ambiguity of her tirade, where she supposedly reports what she told them that they said to her when they were drunk, provides Chaucer with an opportunity to express ideas and feelings, keeping the reader uncertain whether they are Alison's, her husbands', or purely imaginary. Lines 293–302, for example, tell how Alison would like to be treated, and she urges her husbands to set her free from spying and other restraints in lines 318–322. In the comic context this desire for freedom could simply mean that she wants to have affairs with other men. The words go further than this, however: her husband should say, 'I knowe yow for a trewe wyf, dame Alys'. Perhaps she craves her husbands' trust, and would become a 'trewe wyf' of her own accord? Certainly these lines show that she longs to be treated with respect, and resents being spied on or treated as a possession.

In the tirade as a whole, there is a relentless attention to detail. For example, the faults of women are catalogued and classified with dreadful thoroughness: 'a povre womman', 'if that she bee riche', 'if that she be fair' and 'if that she bee foul'. Alison's resentment of these insults is fiercely colloquial, and her natural tone suggests stronger feelings than we would expect about insults she has supposedly invented herself. She bursts out:

> With wilde thonder-dynt and firy levene
> Moote thy welked nekke be tobroke!

And her suffering under the chauvinism of this speech is expressed in the weary question:

> Been ther none othere maner resemblances
> That ye may likne your parables to
> But if a sely wyf be oon of tho?

The sincere tone of these outbursts suggests that there are deeper feelings at stake than the mere fun of lying to her husbands about what they never said. We later discover that Alison suffered misogynist persecution from her fifth husband. It is ironic that she eventually meets the very quality she falsely attributed to the first three husbands.

Finally, one other notable development occurs. We have noticed that she uses images of common things and livestock. There is an image of beauty and value in this passage, however, and it coincides with the lingering metre and musical assonance with which she describes Jankyn the page: 'For his crispe heer, shynynge as gold so fyn'. Surrounded as it is with cynicism and vulgarity, the longing for youth and beauty expressed in this line is poignant, and suggests regret for the equal and loving relationship with a man of her own age that she missed when she married old men for money. We will return to the problem of equality of age at other points in this commentary; for the moment we must simply admire the delicacy with which Chaucer begins to sketch the deeper nature of his character.

The fourth husband (lines 452–502)

Alison disposes of her fourth husband in this much shorter section; and even of these fifty lines only half describe her marriage, the other half being digressions about her youth and her feelings on growing old. The space she devotes to this marriage is, therefore, very small indeed. It is startling, however, in introducing a new phase in the revelation of her character. So far her narrative and the exposition of her views have proceeded logically, for both in arguments and story she has completed everything she began. We have noticed signs of deeper feelings in her, contradicting her public cynicism, but these are still only an undercurrent. When she tells about her last two husbands, however, this undercurrent breaks into the narrative in several ways. She begins to describe an episode, digresses suddenly, and never finishes what she began to say; or the narrative moves forwards and backwards in time, sometimes contradicting itself. At other times she appears to be swept away in sudden rushes of feeling, or veers from idealism to cynicism in the space of two or three lines. Chaucer here introduces a new aspect of the Wife: she is no longer a skilled performer with easy control of argument and audience. Now she begins to struggle to keep her narrative and philosophy coherent, by denying and controlling her own wayward emotions. At the same time she outgrows the medieval convention of a comic figure, and develops the ironic complexity of a modern character.

Alison's startling change is apparent from the first two lines of this passage. Most uncharacteristically she lacks frankness: she calls her fourth husband a 'revelour' – a man who pursues pleasure – but in the next line we realise that this word sidesteps the issue. What she meant to say was that he kept a mistress, 'he hadde a paramour'. We sense that Alison finds his unfaithfulness difficult to talk about even after so many years, and this reluctance led her to use the euphemism 'revelour'. This impression is confirmed when she immediately changes the subject and talks about her youth.

The picture she paints is of a jolly young woman full of fun, music and energy, and she compares herself to a 'pye' and a 'nyghtyngale' – in contrast to the livestock of the last section – recalling spring, freedom and flight. She was also, as she recalls with aggressive alliteration, 'stibourn and strong' and full of passion. In the course of this description, however, she suddenly takes up the subject of wine. The reference to Metellus, another learned example of marital discord, this time from a handbook on rhetoric by Valerius Maximus, strikes a sudden contrast with the previous lines, reintroducing the familiar degrading images: 'the foule cherl, the swyn'. Though startling, this change of mood is only momentary and she goes on to explain that wine is an aphrodisiac:

> A likerous mouth moste han a likerous tayl.
> In wommen vinolent is no defence.

Her final remark that 'lecchours' take advantage of this weakness suggests that her fourth husband was a 'lecchour' who thus took advantage of her, so by a circuitous route she returns to the experiences of her own life.

Alison describes her own youth and declares how she enjoys remembering her jollity. She is satisfied with the life she has lived because 'I have had my world as in my tyme', but is immediately attacked by the other feeling that accompanies nostalgia: regret. The next six lines make a powerful statement on old age and reveal that Alison's feelings about it are in painful turmoil. Age will poison – 'envenyme' – everything, she says bitterly; she regrets her loss of beauty and the vital energy which she calls her 'pith'. She consigns her lost joys sadly to the devil, however, and with obstinate determination returns to a commercial image: she must now sell herself as inferior goods, 'the bren, as I best kan, now moste I selle', echoing the degrading self-images of much earlier in the text. Finally, she seems to say that she can still laugh and enjoy herself. These few lines, then, express a vivid explosion of regret, bitterness and determination to carry on laughing at life. For the first time, however, we sense that she laughs because she must: because she cannot bear to remember seriously the youth she has lost.

The final phase in Alison's account of her fourth marriage returns to the story where she left it: he had a mistress. Now she tells the pilgrims how deeply his unfaithfulness hurt her:

> I seye, I hadde in herte greet despit
> That he of any oother had delit.

Having brought herself to acknowledge this weakness she quickly returns to the attack, asserting that 'he was quit, by God and by seint Joce!' However, the remainder of this passage does not convince us that she subdued her fourth husband, and raises more questions than it answers.

She quickly claims that she was revenged on this husband: she tortured him with jealousy so that only God and he knew 'how soore I hym twiste'. This claim is necessary to her main thesis that she dominated all five husbands, so women must and should have 'soveraynetee' in marriage. On the other hand, she shows uncharacteristic modesty: she was never unfaithful to her fourth husband herself. She says she made him jealous, but 'nat of my body, in no foul manere'. The surprising point about this is that she bothers to say it at all. When describing the first three marriages, Alison strongly hinted at her own adultery and showed no moral shame. Indeed, she boasted that:

> I koude pleyne, and yit was in the gilt,
> Or elles often tyme hadde I been spilte.

Why does she now bother to point out that she feigned adultery without actually committing the sin?

Second, Alison informs us that her husband died when she returned from Jerusalem. We know from 'The General Prologue' that she went to Jerusalem three times, and visited many other shrines in different parts of Europe also. In the Middle Ages travelling was a time-consuming business, and the journeys Alison undertook must have occupied several years. Her passing reference to Jerusalem here indicates that she travelled during this fourth marriage, and the context of his unfaithfulness and her suffering suggests that she went abroad to get away from his neglect. This not only explains how she came to be so well-travelled (only the Knight among the pilgrims could claim more extensive knowledge of the world); it also casts doubt on her claim that she gained 'soveraynetee' over this husband. Her absence just before his death suggests they were still fighting a battle for supremacy in the marriage, that neither of them could ultimately win.

In the end her feelings about this fourth husband are ambivalent. She apologises for the plainness of his grave, raising a surprisingly grandiose comparison between him and Darius, the ancient Persian emperor. With typical bathos she then points out that it is a waste of money to spend on the dead. Next, she wishes him well, 'God yeve his soul reste', in a wistful tone that conveys the idea of her liking him even though they fought all the time. The falseness of Alison's first heavy ironies begins to show through here. She felt only contempt for the three 'goode' husbands, and shows respect and some affection for this, the first of the 'badde' ones.

In this passage, then, contradictions in Alison's character become more powerful and break through into her narrative and argument. Notice particularly the romantic idealism in comparing her husband to Darius, immediately followed by callous pragmatism as she saves money on his funeral. The sense that her warmest feelings are ruthlessly repressed by her cynical habit of mind is most vividly conveyed by this contrast. We also sense that Alison is repressing her feelings when she plunges into her long digression.

This passage is very short and gives few details of the fourth marriage. Readers sometimes fail to notice that this marriage lasted longer than the others. When they married she was 'yong and ful of ragerye'. We soon learn that she married her fifth husband when she was forty, so although she does not specify her age at the beginning of this fourth marriage it seems reasonable to guess that it lasted fifteen years or more: long enough for her to change from a young girl to a middle-aged woman. This reflection is important, as we will see when discussing the theme of old age; and it goes a long way to explain the tumultuous feelings about growing old that are expressed in lines 474–9.

The courtship of Alison and Jankyn (lines 503–626)

We are familiar with the cynical philosophy Alison tries to project, and it is apparent from her account of the fourth husband that this projection is belied by some of her feelings. In this section her vulnerability is further revealed, and revelation alternates with digressions that attempt to shore up her crumbling self-image with increasing wildness and inconsistency.

Her first digression occurs when she mentions her 'gossib' who lived in the town, and returns to the familiar theme of how badly she treated her husband. In this case she refers to her fourth husband, and in the passage between lines 531 and 542 she explains with relish how she told his shameful secrets to others in order to embarrass him. Here Alison is in her most comfortable element. She hints at her wickedness, suggesting that she told her friend secrets she could never confess to a priest; she chooses an outrageous example for her husband's misdeed – that he had 'pissed on a wal' – and thoroughly enjoys his discomfiture as his face becomes 'reed and hoot for verray shame' while she teases him.

After telling of the Lenten walks with Jankyn and her 'gossib', Alison digresses into a pasage celebrating her wildness. Lines 550–62 explain how she behaved behind her husband's back. While he was away at London she went out to every available gathering:

> To vigilies and processiouns;
> To prechyng eek, and to thise pilgrimages,
> To pleyes of myracles, and to mariages.

She wears her brightest and gayest clothes – 'my gaye scarlet gytes' – because she goes to be looked at by people. In contrast to her own exuberance she cites 'wormes', 'motthes' and 'mytes', creatures that evoke paleness and closed cupboards, and which have no chance against her energies.

The next cynical passage follows her account of conversations with Jankyn, and concerns her fourth husband's funeral. Here, Alison is again in her element, presenting herself as shockingly unmoved by her husband's death, and adding the high farce of falling in love with Jankyn's legs as he follows the coffin. She claims that she wept because it is a customary, 'As wyves mooten, for it is usage', and she admits that there were no real tears, only a pretence of grief while 'my coverchief covered my visage'. Her feelings were entirely selfish: she had nothing to be sad about because she was already provided with a husband – 'purveyed of a make'. The word 'make', or mate, recalls the comparison with mating animals she has recurrently used, and the emphasis on physical desire is enhanced by her manner of falling in love. The satire on sentimentality is at its sharpest as she gives her 'herte' to Jankyn's legs. These passages conjure the aggressive and cynical comic entertainer we met at the beginning of the Prologue. They alternate with more controversial and contradictory passages that tell of her courtship with Jankyn.

Alison begins her description of him with a contradiction: she wishes him well, yet he treated more cruelly than did any of the others, and even beat her: 'That feele I on my ribbes al by rewe'. The contradiction is compounded by the next few lines which describe his ability to win her over with his charming talk, however cruelly he had beaten her just before. Alison here frankly admits that she was in Jankyn's power. He mistreated her and controlled her just as she previously mistreated and controlled her first three husbands. Compare, for example, the effect of Jankyn's charm, with the way Alison goaded her old husbands into fury only to charm them back to smiles (see lines 429–50).

The Wife then applies her theories to explain this state of affairs, using the same wisdom that she previously deployed to dominate her husbands. The theory is simply this: that love withheld is desired, while love possessed is no longer wanted. She loved Jankyn best 'for that he was of his love daungerous to me'. Women are like that:

> Forbede us thyng, and that desiren wee;
> Presse on us faste, and thanne wol we fle.

The echo of her former statements becomes even more exact as she resorts to commercial images for desire again:

> Greet prees at market maketh deere ware,
> And to greet cheep is holde at litel prys.

This opening description of Jankyn says frankly that the position of her first three marriages was reversed. He held absolute power over her body and her heart.

When she has acknowledged this weakness she restores her confidence with a digression about embarrassing her fourth husband, but soon the narrative calls her again, and she begins to describe her first meetings with Jankyn. He was her friend's lodger, a clerk from Oxford, and the three of them walked in the fields together in the spring. Suddenly Alison digresses again, enhancing the reader's feeling that she is uneasy about these memories. They are too personal for her to relate in a light-hearted way. This time the digression concerns how she went out while her husband was away. Finally, with sudden decision, she declares, 'Now wol I tellen forth what happed me', and explains what took place during the Lenten walks with Jankyn.

Alison's justification gathers strength as she talks. She begins by saying that she and Jankyn had such loving conversations – 'swich daliance' – that she reserved him then and there for her next husband. This fits her previous statement that she was the weaker partner: now we learn that she proposed to him. However, she glosses this with a cynical explanation, insisting that she always kept more than one man in reserve. Again, her cynicism is expressed in animal images: this time she figures as a 'mouse' that is too sensible to have 'but oon hole for to sterte to, and if that faille, thanne is al ydo'.

Describing their conversations, Alison again adds a cynical gloss to facts that reveal her weakness. She said that he had enchanted her, and claimed that she dreamed of him killing her in bed, so filling the bed with blood. This was clearly a sexual dream, with a nuance on 'slayn' that was current in Chaucer's time, and told him in effect that she loved and needed him desperately. To fit this astonishing admission to her cynical self-image, Alison simply tells us that it was all a trick: she 'bar hym on honde' that she loved him, and the dream 'was fals; I dremed of it right naught'. She was following her mother's advice, lying to trap a man: 'My dame taughte me that soutiltee', and 'I folwed ay my dames loore'. In this case her mother's advice – which she always followed – was the opposite of her usual behaviour.

The effort of talking about Jankyn, and trying to make their courtship fit her aggressive image, must have been considerable. Certainly Alison shows signs of being disturbed by her memories. Her speech becomes broken as she tries to regain the thread of what she was saying:

> But now, sire, lat me se, what I shal seyn?
> A ha! by God, I have my tale ageyn.'

There follows the farcical description of her fourth husband's funeral, when she fell in love with Jankyn's legs.

The final passage in this part of her narrative uses astrology to explain the contradictions in her character. The reversal from her first three marriages is neatly completed by a mention of their ages: Jankyn is twenty and Alison forty. Then she explains her own horoscope. She is the result of astrological contradictions, a character dominated equally by Venus (goddess of love) and Mars (god of war). She has the physiological marks of these two influences also, having birthmarks both on her face and 'in another privee place' – probably near her genitals – which she calls 'the prente of Seinte Venus seel' and 'Martes mark'. The horoscope, she explains, means that she was born when the zodiacal sign of Taurus, which is subject to Venus, pleasure-loving and sensual, was rising ('myn ascendent'), and was consequently powerful; and so Venus gave Alison her 'lust' and 'likerousnesse'. However, the planet Mars was in Taurus at the time, and its influence towards aggression and dominance intercepts and conflicts with Venus's characteristics. So, Mars is responsible for Alison's 'sturdy hardynesse'.

The description of her personality that surrounds this horoscope, however, emphasises the 'Venusian' side of her character: her sexual appetite is so powerful that she cannot restrain her promiscuity. She could never withdraw her 'chambre of Venus' from a 'good felawe'; and she lay with any man. She again asserts her youth, energy and passion and links these with a compliment paid to her by her husbands: that she had the best 'quoniam' (Latin for 'whereas' but here a euphemism for her sexual organs). This outburst of fun and sensuality, containing the contradictory horoscope, comes straight after the final and most disturbing revelation about her and Jankyn: that he was half her age. This part of the Prologue, then, provides further evidence of Alison's volatile moods and the disruption of her narrative as she veers between contradictory feelings; and in the end provides an astrological scheme that symbolises the basic problem of her personality.

The fifth husband (lines 627–828)

This part of the Prologue purports to tell us of a quarrel between Alison and Jankyn, her fifth husband, when she was hit so hard on the ear that she is still deaf. However, as we have come to expect by this time, the narrative begins no less than four times, three of these being false starts leading to digressions. Her digressions all take the same form, retailing the tales of 'wikked wyves' Jankyn read from his book, so I shall treat them together after discussing what we learn about the fifth husband from the passages in between.

Alison's fifth marriage was the reverse of her first three. She made over to Jankyn 'al the lond and fee that evere was me yeven ther bifoore', on the occasion of their wedding. She adds that he was determined to have authority over her, 'He nolde suffre nothyng of my list', and she regretted handing him the financial power. The main point about Jankyn's character revealed in this passage, however, is his fondness for preaching and his interminable proverbs – more 'than in this world ther growen gras or herbes'. Alison would not submit to his authority, and this drove him wild with anger, making him 'with me wood al outrely'.

Alison's reaction to this domineering man was to dig in her heels. She again compares herself with an animal, saying she was as stubborn 'as is a leonesse'; and she walks out visiting as she likes, disobeying his commands. She pays no attention to his ancient proverbs – his 'olde sawe' – and ignores his attempts to correct her. As for Alison's feelings under persecution from Jankyn, she mentions two related emotions: 'I hate hym that my vices telleth me', she says; and indeed her exasperation and fury can be sensed both in her outburst against clerks, in lines 686–710, and have been sensed in the power of resentment we noted earlier, when she was supposedly retailing an imaginary speech against her first three husbands. We now realise that the fury she expressed then was part of the anger she feels at being mistreated by Jankyn.

We now come to one of the most celebrated passages of the whole text, where Alison prefigures many ideas recently advanced by the women's liberation movement. She singles out clerks, not men in general, for her fury; but two of her points correspond to those of modern feminism. First, she asserts that books give a biased account of women because they are written by men:

> Who peyntede the leon, tel me who?
> By God! If wommen hadde writen stories,
> As clerkes han withinne hire oratories,
> They wolde han writen of men moore wikkednesse
> Than al the mark of Adam may redresse.

Second, she imputes men's prejudices to their own sexual inadequacy: all the anti-women stories, she says, are the work of impotent old men:

> . . . whan he is oold, and may noght do
> Of Venus werkes worth his olde sho,
> Thanne sit he doun, and writ in his dotage
> That wommen kan nat kepe hire mariage.

Alison links her condemnation of clerks with the astrological influence supposed to dominate the studious life: Mercury. She explains that Mercury is so incompatible with Venus, her own planet, that whenever one rises the other falls. So, having previously explained her own nature in terms of her horoscope, she now turns to astrology to account for the bitter conflicts in her fifth marriage.

Having expressed this anger against Jankyn, misogynists, and clerks in general, she eventually acknowledges that she feels pain. Jankyn's overbearing prejudice against women hurts her. We remember her desire to be told, 'I knowe you for a trewe wyf, Dame Alys'; and we know that she is vulnerable to Jankyn because she wants his love and trust. The immediate cause of her action in tearing pages out of his book is an intensity of suffering that becomes insupportable:

> Who wolde wene, or who wolde suppose,
> The wo that in myn herte was, and pyne?

The married life of Alison and Jankyn before the crucial quarrel was a bitter struggle between two determined personalities, then, and was characterised by his tormenting anti-feminism and her obstinacy and suffering under this treatment. Our picture of their life together comes in fragments as Alison tries to narrate the story of their quarrel: it is revealed in intervals between batches of the tales about 'wikked wyves' that Jankyn read so interminably.

Chaucer's choice of a learned clerk for Alison's fifth husband both provides the occasion for her attack on the anti-feminism of the Church, and explains her own incongruous learning, which is a rich element in the heady mix of her personality. We have noticed her familiarity with 'auctoritee' earlier, and enjoyed Alison's and Chaucer's exploitation of the ironies between her scholarship and her own earthy common sense. Now we discover that this learning, that she used to such devastating comic effect, was acquired through suffering. Jankyn the clerk had a book which he called 'Valerie and Theofraste'. This was a compilation of anti-feminist tracts from various authors, as the Wife explains.

'Valerie' refers to the 'Epistola Valerii . . . etc.' of Walter Map, and 'Theofraste' was the 'Liber de Nuptiis' or 'book of marriages' by Theophrastus. Both of these are miscellanies in which the failings of women are described and satirised. Also included in Jankyn's volume is Saint Jerome's tract against Jovinian, a monk of the fifth century who was condemned for holding the opinion that virginity is not a higher state than marriage. Saint Jerome was one of the most respected early Christian scholars, a notable 'auctoritee'. 'Tertulan' is probably Tertullian, another early Christian who wrote treatises on monogamy, chastity and modesty. 'Crisippus, Trotula and Helowys' are more difficult to fit into Jankyn's collection. 'Crisippus' is mentioned ambiguously by Jerome, Trotula may have been a female doctor specialising in gynaecology in eleventh-century Salerno, but scholars are uncertain of the reference; and 'Helowys' was Eloise, the secret wife of Abelard from the celebrated story, who eventually became a prioress. The ambiguity of these three references may indicate that Alison is joking with her audience. To take Eloise alone, the prioress who was famous for her passionate love is an ambiguous figure: perhaps Alison refers to her to remind the pilgrims of the passions that always exist under a veneer of holiness? Two other contributors to Jankyn's book are mentioned: Solomon for the book of Proverbs, and Ovid for 'Ars Amatoria' ('the art of love'), a satirical work giving mock advice on how to succeed in love. We can see how the proverbs and Ovid's anecdotes suit Jankyn's anti-women collection; but at the same time these 'auctoritees' are double-edged. Either Jankyn was so doctrinaire and simple-minded that he took these works at face value; or Alison, in gaining her learning at second-hand, did not appreciate the ironies of her more learned husband. We know from Alison's mistake about Midas, that Jankyn was not above misquoting his sources to her, distorting the truth to suit his purpose.

Jankyn read this 'book of wikked wyves' for pleasure, 'gladly', and he turned to it 'alway'. He 'lough alwey ful faste' and used the book whenever 'he hadde leyser and vacacioun from oother worldly occupacioun'. We would be dull to miss the implication of these reinforcing phrases: that Jankyn enjoyed tormenting his wife with a recitation of woman's frailty.

Our first direct taste of Jankyn's preaching comes in lines 642–58. Alison lists stories of Ancient Rome that Jankyn cited, of Simplicius Gallus who left his wife because he once saw her stand bareheaded at the door; and of another Roman whose wife went out to a 'someres game' – a midsummer festival – causing him to leave her. Both of these are from the Roman historian Valerius Maximus, evidently another source in Jankyn's book. Alison next gives a sample, from her husband's collection of proverbs, and caricatures the relentless sing-song of his speeches with four contrived rhyme-words in a row: 'salwes . . . falwes . . . halwes . . . galwes'. The didactic nonsense of Jankyn's proverbs is set off by her return to natural speech in the next line: 'But al for nought, I sette not an hawe. . .'.

The larger slice of Jankyn's speech we find between lines 715 and 785 contains a number of references, the majority of them drawn from the 'Epistola Valerii' or Saint Jerome. 'Eva' was Eve, the first woman in the Bible's book of Genesis, who is supposed to have caused the fall of the human race by leading her husband Adam into temptation. The story of Samson and Delilah is mentioned next, followed by that of Hercules, whose wife Deianira gave him the shirt of Nessus to revive his love for her, not knowing that it was poisoned. Hercules allowed his body to be consumed by fire to escape the agony of the poisoned shirt. The ancient Greek philosopher Socrates comes next, with an anecdote culled from Jerome about his marital troubles, then Jankyn moves on to Pasiphae from Greek mythology, who mated with a bull and gave birth to the half bull Minotaur. Next we are told about Clytemnestra, wife of Agamemnon who commanded the Greeks at the siege of Troy. She took a lover while Agamemnon was at Troy and when he returned she murdered him in his bath with an axe. The story of Imphiaraus and his wife Eriphyle is that she accepted a bribe to persuade him to join a war against Thebes in which he was killed. 'Lyvia' was Livia who conspired with her lover Sejanus to poison her husband Drusus in Rome; and 'Lucye' was Lucilia, wife of the Roman poet and philosopher Lucretius. Finally, Jankyn tells a story from 'Epistola Valerii' about a Roman called Latumius whose friend Arrius begged him for a cutting from the 'blessed' tree on which three of his wives had hanged themselves.

Alison sketches the rest of Jankyn's preaching, saying that he had a stock of other stories from more recent times – 'of latter date' – and that he knew more proverbs against women than you could imagine. Most of the proverbs she mentions derive from the books of Ecclesiastes and Proverbs in the Bible, and bring us to the end of

Jankyn's sermon against women. We should notice the Wife's style in this passage, however, before moving on.

First, this sample of anti-feminist stories is laced with Alison's own colloquial language. For example, Delilah is described with a common endearment as Samson's 'lemman', and she cut his hair with shears; and Socrates' wife threw 'pisse' on his head, while Alison plainly enjoys Socrates' comment on this: 'Er that thonder stynte, comth a reyn!' The effect is that Alison's vitality and earthy fun are added to this display of learning, mocking the pompous erudition of clerks by pointing out in this way that their books consist merely of funny and scurrilous stories. Second, Jankyn's speech gathers pace as the full examples are left behind in line 764, giving way to brief references, generalisations about the innumerable stories he knew and finally a series of proverbs separated by only one or two words. The way the passage accelerates creates the sense of pressure building to a climax that precedes Alison's outburst, and helps to convey the intolerable strain she is under.

This build-up of tension leads straight into an account of the quarrel itself, which Alison at last narrates without digression. It is the climax of the Wife's Prologue; and what happens in this quarrel is crucial to the character she has projected from the start. Alison has explained her cynical outlook and remained true to her thesis that women should have 'soveraynetee' in marriage. She manipulated love, desire and jealousy to her own advantage through four marriages, but disastrously departed from her own precepts in two ways when she married Jankyn. First, she allowed herself to desire him too much so he held the sexual advantage; and second, she gave him financial power by surrendering all her property when they married. We remember how difficult it was for Alison to admit her lapse, and how she tried to gloss her weakness as strength by contradicting herself. In Jankyn she meets her match, and she has a chance to recover from her mistake: the quarrel is crucial, then, both to their marriage and to the purpose of Alison's life. This is what happens.

The Wife cannot bear Jankyn's endless sermon against women. She tears 'thre leves' from his book and hits him on the cheek with her fist so hard that he 'fil bakward adoun' into the fire. He leaps up like a mad lion and punches her on the head so hard she falls down and lies still. Jankyn is scared of what he has done and thinks of running away, but the Wife wakes up and accuses him of murdering her for her land. Then she adds:

Er I be deed, yet wol I kisse thee

Jankyn kneels and begs her forgiveness, but she takes advantage of his proximity to hit him again 'on the cheke'. She then says she will die. But, she tells the pilgrims, 'atte laste' and 'with muchel care and wo' they came to an agreement. He gave her 'soveraynetee': the power to decide what he should say and do, and power over their property. He also agreed to burn his book of 'wikked wyves' straight away. In giving her 'soveraynetee' he adjures her to 'keep thyn honour, and keep eek myn estaat'; in other words he asks her to look after their reputation. Alison says she was a 'kynde' and 'trewe' wife to him from then on, and he was true to her. On this note of perfect marital harmony she concludes her narrative with a blessing on Jankyn, and announces that she will now tell her tale.

Two points arise from the quarrel, which both concern the central question: how far should we believe Alison's account of what happened? First, Alison tells us about the quarrel in a character-istically ambiguous manner. In particular, there is a contrast. Evident ambiguity in 'I lay *as* I were deed' and 'atte laste out of my swogh I breyde'; sentimental melodrama in 'Er I be deed, yet wol I kisse thee', and high comedy in 'eftsoones I hitte hym on the cheke' followed by absurd melodrama in 'Now wol I dye, I may no lenger speke': all these tell a cynical story of Alison manipulating Jankyn's feelings in a scene of knockabout farce. On the other hand, the plainness of Alison's narrative in lines 788–95, the balanced sincerity of Jankyn's submission and his plea for respectability, and the moving sincerity with which Alison asks God's blessing on his soul 'for his mercy deere': all these suggest that the quarrel was an emotional crisis, an important experience in Alison's life.

The second point is prompted by this contrast of styles: is the Wife simultaneously giving two different versions of the quarrel? Earlier, Alison comically claimed that she fell in love with Jankyn's legs at her husband's funeral, contradicting what she revealed before, that she fell in love when walking in the fields while her husband was away. Which version is true? In this case, the cynical high comedy comes when she tricks him into coming near, and then hits him again; yet afterwards, somehow, they were reconciled. We are entitled to ask: did she really hit him, or has she embroidered her story for comic effect? A further point should strike the attentive reader: Alison gives a blow-by-blow and word-for-word account of their quarrel as far as line 810. Then the details suddenly cease and she asserts that they were reconciled 'atte laste'. It is difficult to see how such an aggressive piece of deception as her second punch, could lead to reconciliation and marital harmony. The questions arise from Ali-son's account of the crisis in her fifth marriage. They are difficult questions for any student or critic to unravel, but they lend weight to the view that Alison's repression of her softer feelings might be strong enough to make her distort or hide the truth.

The words between the Summoner and the Friar (lines 829–56)

Alison is interrupted for a second time when the Friar makes a laughing comment on the length of her Prologue. The Summoner complains about this interruption, and slips in an insult about Friars. The Friar promises to tell tales about Summoners, and the Summoner parries with a promise to tell tales about Friars. It takes an intervention from the Host to stop them bickering. He then orders Alison to tell her tale and she assents.

The significance of this passage is twofold. First, it is part of the dramatic context of *The Canterbury Tales*, developing the Friar and the Summoner as characters and providing motivation for their tales, which follow Alison's and make up the remainder of Fragment III of the whole work. We are primarily interested in the other function of this interlude, however, as a sudden break between Alison's Prologue and her Tale.

The Wife has been less and less in control of her own Prologue, revealing her feelings more fully than she intended. The climax of her self-revelation is the account of Jankyn that she has just given. Alison wishes Jankyn well with heartfelt emotion. The Friar's offhand interruption is cruel, and has a bathetic effect. It is a sharp reminder that Alison has a critical audience, and the Friar's attitude contrasts harshly with the nostalgia Alison is in danger of indulging. This, and the quarrel that follows, is a challenge to Alison's control over herself and her audience. She does not respond as quickly as she did when the Pardoner interrupted, indicating that she is taken unawares. Instead it is left to the Host to restore order, and Alison gives only one belated sign that she will rise to the Friar's challenge: her sarcasm in asking his permission to continue with her Tale. She asks him for 'licence' in a pun that ridicules the 'licence' or permit he holds to beg in a 'limit' or area, by which means he dishonestly makes a lot of money.

Chaucer here shows perfect command of characters and tone, puncturing the sentiment that ends the Wife's Prologue, yet in such a way that our sympathy is not reduced; and setting a lighter, more cynical tone for the opening of the Tale without taking away from the realism of Alison's previous revelations. The interruption also displays the skill with which Chaucer matches the rhythms of natural speech to the form of his poetry: we can hear anger growing in the

Friar's voice as his genial façade slips and he shows his real self: 'Ye, woltow so, sire Somonour'; and the Summoner's petulance is neatly conveyed in: 'What! amble, or trotte, or pees, or go sit doun!'

The usefulness of Friars (lines 857–81)

The Wife opens her tale with a conventional acknowledgement that the magic that will figure in her story belongs to 'th'olde dayes of the Kyng Arthour'. Since the coming of Holy Church the old magic of 'fayerie', with all its associated mythical creatures such as elves and fairies, has lost its power and disappeared. This kind of acknowledgement was commonplace before a story of magic or astrology. When the Franklin introduces a magician into his tale, for example, he makes a similar apology:

> . . . and swich folye
> As in oure dayes is nat worth a flye, –
> for hooly chirches feith in our bileve
> Ne suffreth noon illusioun us to greve. (Robinson, p. 139)

In Chaucer's time the Church was still fighting the influence of the old religion, that relic of beliefs in magic and nature-worship that was still strong in country areas. Alison gives her tale respectability by bowing to the great goodness of the Church in ridding England of witches, before she indulges the delight of a story about magic. It is worth noting that nature-worship has a way of surviving its suppression: it is alive today in Christmas trees, mistletoe, maypoles and the enduring attraction of Robin Hood, as well as in a hundred other ways.

It is no surprise, therefore, that the Wife begins in this way. However, her mock-gratitude to the Church marks the emphatic return of the Wife we met at the beginning of her Prologue. She is again saucy, savouring every sexual innuendo, and she reaffirms her control over the audience in devastating fashion. She simply chooses to thank Friars instead of the Church as a whole. Warming to her subject, she conjures a world infested with Friars 'As thikke as motes in the sonne-beem', and hiding 'in every bussh or under every tree'. This is clearly aimed at Huberd the 'limitour' who interrupted so rudely. The Friar's portrait in 'The General Prologue' stresses his cruelty, greed and lechery. The Wife concentrates on his lechery, implying that he seduces ladies and servants with equal abandon, in her comprehensive list of the places he 'blesses'. She goes on to say that where the old wicked spirit called an 'incubus' was dangerous because it invariably caused pregnancy, the Friar is safe: he will only bring dishonour on the women he meets. This not only implies that Friars rape every woman they sight, but also perhaps that Friars are sterile; and the Wife is not too shy to conjure an outrageous picture of safe intercourse: 'Wommen may go now saufly up and doun.'

There are also more serious stings in this passage. Alison compares Friars to specks in a sunbeam, suggesting perhaps that they obstruct the light of God. The comparison with an 'incubus' implies criticism of Huberd's function as a parasite on society. Finally, she crushingly puns the title 'limitour', saying that the Friar walks 'in his lymyta-cioun'. We can guess that Huberd the Friar is feeling very uncomfort-able by the time Alison finishes with him, and the rest of the pilgrims are probably laughing aloud at his expense.

The knight's crime and the queen's sentence (lines 882–918)

Alison's Tale is a conventional folk-tale, a form of entertainment the pilgrims are all familiar with. She quickly disposes of the prelimina-ries. A young knight rapes a girl he meets alone on the road, he is condemned to death for this crime, but the queen and other ladies beg the king to be merciful and the king gives the rapist into the queen's power. As Alison relates this part of the story there is barely any sign of the lively and varied voice, full of vitality and double meanings, that makes her attack on Friars so funny. With the possible exception of the vigorous verb 'rafte' describing the rape itself, this narration does not sound characteristic of the Wife, and some critics have taken this and other variations of style in the Tale as a sign that Chaucer failed to adapt the story sufficiently to suit Alison's cha-racter.

Be that as it may, the Wife's own voice is re-established as the queen passes sentence, so any lapse on Chaucer's part is short-lived. The queen puts a life-question to the knight, asking him to tell her 'What thyng is it that wommen moost desiren'. The arrogant young knight is about to answer, but she rushes to stop him, saying 'Be war, and keep thy nekke-boon from iren!' then she allows him the customary year and a day to find the answer.

The young knight who will eventually yield 'soveraynetee' to his wife, then, begins with a crime that is the epitome of male 'maistrye'. We should also note that the queen's question can be answered from her own behaviour: she begs the king to give her power over life and death, and when she has the case 'al at hir wille, /To chese wheither she wolde hym save or spille', then she 'thanketh the kyng with al hir myght'. This little portrait of royal life echoes Jankyn's submission and subsequent happiness from the Prologue, and neatly reinforces the case for women's 'soveraynetee'.

The knight searches for an answer (lines 919–88)

The allotted year passes and the knight travels trying to discover 'What thyng is it that wommen moost desiren'. His hopeless quest gives Alison an opportunity to expound her views on women's desires, and she does so with characteristic energy. In this section, Chaucer sets a tone of confident comedy with the command of audience that we remember from the early parts of the Wife's Prologue.

The Friar's interruption was a shock to Alison. It shattered the intimate mood that the story of her life with Jankyn had fostered. Perhaps she was temporarily lost for words while the Host restored order, but she recovered quicky and attacked the Friar. Here, the cynical philosophy of the early Prologue returns, making Alison strong again, irreverent and outrageously funny; while the dangerous sentimentality and contradictions of the latter part of her Prologue are put aside. This is noticeable, first, in her style, which returns to its wonted volatility. She passes easily from ironic description of a woman's steadfastness in this balanced couplet:

> And in o purpos stedefastly to dwelle,
> And nat biwreye thyng that men us telle.

to this sudden exclamation:

> But that tale is nat worth a rake-stele.
> Pardee, . . .

The common images of the early Prologue also return. Women caught by flattery are like trapped birds, 'ylymed', and the behaviour of animals appears as women 'kike' men who scratch them on a sore spot, or 'clawe us on the galle'. The 'rake-stele' or rake-handle reminds us of wooden bowls and other household implements from the Prologue, and even Midas's wife is a marsh-bird putting her beak into the muddy water.

The story of Midas is triumphant high comedy again. Alison introduces it abruptly, interrupting her Tale to ask whether the pilgrims want to hear another story, 'Wol ye heere the tale?' She is at her best as she describes the intolerable pressure of a secret in Midas's wife's heart. The image of this burden which 'swal so soore aboute hir herte' builds up until her heart is 'a-fyre' and she blurts out the scandalous truth. The iambic metre is broken twice in the next line, with two emphatic 'Nows' in which we hear the gasp of relief the woman releases as soon as the secret is out.

Chaucer also links this passage and the Prologue in content. The list of things that women might desire in lines 925–28 echoes her old husbands' lists of female attractions (lines 257–61) even to the same rhyme-word – 'richesse' – and contains a typically self-denigrating reference to her own five marriages. She then focuses on four of women's possible desires, that also strike chords in our memory of the Prologue: that women enjoy flattery and attention, recalling her husbands' complaints about the respectful treatment she demands in lines 293–302; that women should be free to do as they like, which is what she tells her old husbands to say to her (see line 318), and which is also important in Jankyn's submission (see lines 819–20); that women hate to be criticised and will 'kike' the man who tells them the truth about themselves, echoing her complaint about Jankyn's preaching ('I hate hym that my vices telleth me'); and finally the story of Midas recalls how she told all her friends that her husband had 'pissed on a wal', and reminds us that:

> Deceite, wepyng, spynnyng God hath yive
> To wommen kyndely, whil that they may lyve.

Chaucer has filled this passage with echoes of the cynical themes of the Prologue, and in doing so he re-establishes the Wife's more confident voice.

As we know from the Prologue, Alison in this mood is commanding and hilarious, but limited. There is a reminder of the errors inherent in her views when her learning again lets her down. In Ovid's story it was Midas's barber, not his wife, who betrayed the secret of his ears. Alison, probably innocently, repeats Jankyn's distortion here. Her aggression may defend her against her own inner doubts but it cannot cope with the full range of human learning and experience.

The 'Olde Wyf', the answer and the court (lines 989–1103)

In this part of the Tale several different elements coalesce: Alison's character, her main theme of 'soveraynetee', developing ideas about poverty, old age and 'gentillesse', and the folk-story she tells, all become intertwined. It is a very complex mixture.

Some critics argue that Chaucer fails to match the styles of Tale and Prologue. In his introduction to the Cambridge edition, for example, James Winny says that the idiom of the 'tale proper' is 'more restrained' and he detects a 'courtly narrator replaced the

Wife' (*The Wife of Bath's Prologue and Tale* (Cambridge University Press, 1965) p. 23). You can decide this question for yourself, but there is no obvious lapse on Chaucer's part. Some lines are splendidly colloquial, fitting excited speech to the constraints of verse as naturally as any in the Prologue:

> 'Nay, thanne,' quod she, 'I shrewe us bothe two!'

or

> 'My love?' quod he, 'nay, my dampnacioun!'

Such lines, together with the build-up through verbal irony to farce as the knight's misery reaches its crescendo in the marriage bed where 'He walweth and he turneth to and fro', show that Chaucer is as fully in charge of the dramatic situation here as he is elsewhere. James Winny seems too glib in ascribing faults to Chaucer; but it is important to know that the controversy exists.

The Wife's main interest in her Tale is the theme of 'soveraynetee' in love, which is both the answer to the life-question and the catalyst that magically effects a happy ending. This is the central doctrine she advances in both Prologue and Tale. The development of this theme in the present passage is clear. First the 'olde wyf' is offered payment ('I wolde wel quite youre hire') but money is not enough and she demands power: he must promise to be at her command in anything that lies in his 'myght' to do. When his answer is judged to be right, the hag immediately asserts the 'soveraynetee' he gave her with his promise, demanding that he marry her. He again offers money, but she persists and extends her claim to power: she will be both his 'wyf' and also his 'love'. He ridicules this new idea; it will be disastrous to have to marry her, but the idea that he could love such a common old woman is utterly absurd. On their wedding night she still demands his love. She is 'smylynge everemo' because she enjoys his discomfiture, but the point of her taunting speech is that he must not only be her husband but also make love to her. So Alison of Bath steadily develops the theme of 'soveraynetee', explaining what is meant by the knyght's answer to the court:

> Wommen desiren to have sovereynetee
> As wel over hir housbond as hir love.

The comedy of the whole situation is enhanced by Alison's character-istic interpretation of love as lust, bereft of the romantic associations we often attach to the word. It is just possible that the knight would feel a bond of attachment – on some level – for the woman who saved his life. In Alison's scheme of things, however, human beings are reduced to their instinctive functions, and love is synonymous with sex. This is emphasised by the old wife's teasing and the ambiguous use of 'dangerous', even more bitingly ironic in the light of his original crime of rape. It is, of course, impossible for him to be physically attracted to the hag.

The Wife's doctrine of 'soveraynetee' and her cynical treatment of love have raised the same question in both her narratives: what kind of man would submit to her? In the Prologue we meet several distinctive male characters, but the most vivid creation was Jankyn, with his masculine charm and misogynist obsession. Alison's account does not convincingly explain how this strong tyrant is transformed into a submissive lover.

We can consider the knight in the light of these thoughts: what kind of a man does Alison imagine him to be? He began by raping a girl, a direct challenge to the female 'soveraynetee' the Wife has in mind. When sentenced he thought he could answer straight away, and when warned against that, he hoped that God would help him. Several points are now added to his portrait. When he sees 'foure and twenty' ladies dancing, he approaches them eagerly. The sexual eagerness that led to his crime a year before is still present, even now when he is in despair. When the illusory dance disappears, however, and the hag bars his way, he addresses her courteously as 'my leeve mooder'. Alison emphasises the point that he has learned some manners, at least, by dwelling on the hag's repulsive appearance: 'A fouler wight ther may no man devyse'.

When the old wife demands his hand, his character further emerges. He makes no pretence of willingness, but his words reveal snobbery more than any other trait. The old wife itemises three objections – that she is 'foul, and oold, and poore' – but he is overwhelmed by the shame of her low birth:

> Allas! that any of my nacioun
> Sholde evere so foule disparaged be!

The emphasis is on his 'nacioun' – his family – and on the social opprobrium of 'disparaged'. When they are in their marriage bed he acknowledges that she is 'loothly' and 'oold', but his main objection is again against her birth:

> And therto comen of so lough a kynde

The knight, then, is a social snob, and the development of this idea leads naturally into the sermon on 'gentillesse' in the hag's subsequent speech. Surprisingly, it seems that her age is more of an objection to her than it is to him, while he never mentions her poverty at all.

The hag's character is also worth looking at. Her position in the story invites comparison with Alison of Bath; and at this point in the Tale she displays some of the characteristics of Alison. At the same time, however, she is different from her author. For example, her burgeoning demands in the name of 'soveraynetee' are typical of Alison, as is her enjoyment of the young knight's agony in bed; and she teases him sexually as Alison once goaded her three old husbands. On the other hand she dismisses wealth:

> I nolde for al the metal, ne for oore,
> That under erthe is grave, or lith above. . .

and she prefers marriage and love. This reminds us of Alison's lapse when she married Jankyn, but is not in tune with the woman who charged her husbands a 'raunson' for her sexual favours and won back all her wealth in the end. In addition, the old wife justifies herself in terms Alison would not have used:

> What is my gilt? For Goddes love, tel me it,
> And it shal been amended, if I may.

The bewildered and earnest tone of this may echo Alison's desperation in lines 786–7 or the sincerity of lines 368–70, but does not reflect the dominant philosophy of the Prologue. Some critics see this inconsistency between Alison and the old wife as another sign of Chaucer's failure to sustain his dramatic creation from the Prologue through to the Tale.

Two elements of the fairy story itself are worth noting: the greenwood scene, and the court of ladies where the queen presides. The twenty-four ladies who attract the knight into a 'forest syde' are obviously an illusion of 'fayerie', but what may be less clear to a modern student are the implications of this little scene. The knight eagerly leaves the road and enters the greenwood. It would not be lost on the medieval audience that he has left a Christian path because his over-hot desires betray him into the wicked power of witchcraft. In case this point is missed, the hag reminds him when she bars his way, that he is on the wrong road: 'heer forth ne lith no wey'.

The court presided over by the queen, and made up of ladies of every kind, is a delightful fantasy of female 'soveraynetee' for Alison of Bath. Such a court also had a parallel in the courts of love reputedly held at Poitiers in the twelfth century by Marie of Champagne and Eleanor of Aquitaine, and celebrated in the influential tract *De Amore* by Andreas Capellanus. These fabled courts decided love cases and were much elaborated in the literature of courtly love, but there is some doubt whether they actually existed; and Chaucer's parodies of courtly lovers elsewhere (see the characters Aurelius in 'The Franklin's Tale', Absalon in 'The Miller's Tale' and Damyan in 'The Merchant's Tale' as examples) show that he was critical of courtly love and believed its idealism to be nothing more than dressed-up lust. The queen's court described here is a parody. The 'love-case' this court tried is not courtly at all, but a brutal case of rape. A year later, the court gives justice to an old hag claiming breach of promise against a young knight – a grotesque example of love indeed! Chaucer subtly adds to his parody of female jurisdiction and courtly love in the words of the hag:

> Lat se which is the proudeste of hem alle,
> That wereth on a coverchief or a calle,

The old wife imagines the pride of courtly ladies in association with their head-dresses. This should remind us that Alison is inordinately proud of her own Sunday headgear. It is a gentle, ironic reminder that this courtly fairy story is told by an aggressive, competitive woman of the provincial mercantile class.

The old wife's speech (lines 1104–218)

Having nagged the knight to specify the reasons for his misery, the old wife answers him in a long speech. She begins with a promise that she can 'amende al this' if he behaves well to her. The remainder of her speech is in the form of a sermon divided under two main headings, 'gentillesse' and poverty, with an added tailpiece about foulness and old age. Before treating these subjects separately, we should look at the sermon as a whole.

The lectures on 'gentillesse' and poverty are written in a conventional style using the language of informed debate, not the heady mix of colloquial and learned styles that we are accustomed to from Alison of Bath. When she says that fire always keeps to its 'office natureel', or that an ancestor's virtue is 'a strange thyng to thy persone', the words 'office', 'strange' and 'persone' are used in a philosophical, learned sense. The unambiguous morality of this style is also uncharacteristic of Alison's voice. The logic of this conclusion:

> Thanne am I gentil, whan that I big ynne
> To lyven vertuously and weyve synne.

shows an unquestioning belief in virtue that bears little relation to the moral chaos of, for example, the opening of the Wife's Prologue.

There are also close echoes of other writings by Chaucer. For these reasons we can conclude that Chaucer inserted into the Wife's Tale a piece of writing that may not have been composed with the Wife of Bath in mind.

On the other hand, notice the skill with which the poet has inserted this passage. The old wife's first remark about 'gentillesse' begins a discussion of the distinction between inherited and innate nobility, the philosophical basis of the whole passage; but the style of these lines is still naturalistic, leading to a typically Alisonian dismissal.

> Swich arrogance is nat worth an hen.

Chaucer introduces his major thematic point before passing into a formal style, thus leading the reader gradually into the 'gentillesse' sermon. Again at the end of the speech, the old wife returns to a naturalistic style by degrees, so we are eased back into Alison's dramatic presence. When the lecture on poverty is over, she appears to open a third topic – 'elde' – in the same learned manner. She makes only one point in this vein, however, before dismissing the sermon with:

> And auctours shal I fynden, as I gesse.

Having abandoned scholarly style with this dismissal of 'auctoritee', Chaucer gives us a swift and humorous reminder of the Wife's Prologue, reviving the discussion of chastity in ugly women from lines 265–70 and contradicting the old husband's supposed opinion:

> For filthe and eelde, also moot I thee,
> Been grete wardeyns upon chastitee.

The arch tone, here, both brings back Alison's dramatic presence, and prepares us for the choice the Knight will be offered between ugly faithfulness and beautiful promiscuity.

Gentillesse

The word 'gentillesse' has no exact modern equivalent; and the development of this term even within *The Canterbury Tales* shows that it was being radically redefined in Chaucer's time. Its nearest equivalents are 'nobility' or 'virtue', and the old wife's main point is that these qualities belong to character, not social rank or birth. She dismisses the medieval view – that a person's quality is determined by their birth – and endorses the modern view that a person's quality is demonstrated in the quality of their life and actions. In other words, she proposes to replace the old order of feudal hierarchy with a new order of meritocracy. In this way, the arguments over 'gentillesse' exemplify the ambivalence of Chaucer's time (see Chapter 1), and it is appropriate that the self-made bourgeoise Alison of Bath puts forward the modern view.

The substance of the argument Chaucer puts forward is found in his moral ballad 'Gentillesse'. There are two related points: first that 'vertu' and 'dignitee' are not inherited, and second that 'vertuous noblesse' belongs naturally to God, who 'maketh hem his heyres that him queme', or bequeaths virtue to those who please him. The bulk of the old wife's speech elaborates these two points, drawing on material from *The Consolations of Philosophy* by Boethius, which Chaucer translated as *Boece*, *The Convivio* of Dante, borrowing several lines almost verbatim from *The Romaunt of the Rose*, and including a brief reference to Valerius Maximus, a source used several times in the Wife's Prologue.

The old wife's argument is in four stages that are better discussed in their logical order rather than the order in which they appear. First, she asserts that qualities belonging 'natureely' (innate qualities) are constant. She cites the example of fire which has natural qualities of heat and light. Fire will burn brightly wherever you put it, even in the:

> . . . derkeste hous
> Bitwix this and the mount of Kaukasous.

By contrast, 'gentillesse' is not innate: we see that nobly born people repeatedly do evil, so 'gentillesse' does not run in aristocratic families. The fire example appears in Boethius, as well as in other authors Chaucer knew.

The second point is deduced from the first. Since 'gentillesse' is not a quality belonging to people 'natureely', it is not hereditary. Our ancestors can pass their possessions to us;

> temporel thyng, that man may hurte and mayme,

but:

> Yet may they nat biquethe, for no thyng,
> To noon of us hir vertuous lyvyng.

The old wife underlines this point by explaining that those looking for 'gentillesse' should not look for noble birth or 'old richesse', but:

> Looke who that is moost vertuous alway,
> Pryvee and apert, and moost entendeth ay
> To do the gentil dedes that he kan.

This explains that a person of low birth can be 'gentil', while the converse is given in an echo of *The Romaunt of the Rose*: 'For vileyns synful dedes make a cherl'. The old wife reinforces her point with a reference to Tullius Hostillius, a Roman mentioned in Valerius Maximus's Roman 'gestes' who rose from poverty to power and riches, and a general appeal to the authority of Seneca and Boethius.

The third stage also follows from the first: if 'gentillesse' is not natural in people, then it comes from God. Chaucer puts an English rendering of lines from Dante's *Convivio* into the old wife's mouth:

> . . . for God, of his goodnesse,
> Wol that of hym we clayme oure gentillesse.

The idea of 'gentillesse' is developed here, echoing the point also made in Chaucer's 'Balade'. If God wishes us to claim our 'gentillesse' from him, it follows that, like life, salvation and grace, 'gentillesse' is part of the infinite bounty of God, as the old wife points out by identifying it with 'grace': 'Thanne comth oure verray gentillesse of grace'.

'Gentillesse', then, is closely identified with Christian virtues like love and mercy, and since it is a natural quality of God it is also a means to salvation. This aspect of 'gentillesse' is later further developed in 'The Franklin's Tale' where three men, for different reasons, demonstrate Christian selflessness in the name of 'gentillesse'.

Finally, the argument is taken a further stage: since virtuous people are 'gentil', the old wife imagines a different way of ordering society, and implies that it is God's will for society to be ordered according to this modern view of 'gentillesse'. The aristocracy became 'gentil' because their ancestors originally possessed the quality of 'gentillesse'. The old wife proposes this when she says that our elders cannot hand down their 'vertuous lyvyng': 'That made hem gentil men ycalled be'.

In addition, Tullius Hostillius's 'gentillesse' was enough to raise him to 'heigh noblesse' at the top of Roman society. So by implication the influence and position gained by virtuous reputation will, in the long run, overthrow the social order of feudalism and inherited wealth.

Poverty and 'elde'

The passage dealing with poverty is amalgamated from aphorisms of Seneca, Dante and Juvenal, and echoes from *The Romaunt of the*

Rose; but it is not constructed as logically as the lecture on 'gentil-lesse' and remains rather a group of references cobbled together. This becomes clear when we look at the style, for the passage consists of couplets and quatrains which are easily separated from each other, being either complete sentences or complete clauses each pointing out a different advantage of poverty.

The old wife says that Christ chose to live in poverty, so it must be a virtuous state; it can also bring happiness: the poor who accept their lot with 'pacience' are free from covetousness and the danger of being robbed, so poverty 'syngeth properly'. In addition, she tells us that poverty is 'hateful good' – that is, although difficult to bear it is good for you. This is supported by several reasons: being poor makes you work hard; it helps you to know yourself and God and so gives you wisdom; and it helps you know who your real friends are. These ideas are neatly expressed in antithetical terms, so that whoever is poor but happy, 'I holde hym riche', while the covetous person is 'a povre wight' and he who does not covet anything 'is riche' even if the world thinks him only a 'knave'. The same play on opposites occurs in 'hateful good', paraphrasing 'Paupertas est odibile bonum', an apho-rism attributed to Secundus that also appears in the contemporary *Piers Plowman* by Langland.

The old wife's final topic is 'elde' or old age, and as she begins to speak of this we are reminded of the dramatic situation. She argues that we are taught to respect our elders, and that ugly old women are necessarily chaste. The second of these points echoes the cynical mood of Alison's Prologue, but our return to dramatic narrative begins with the change to more natural phrasing and sentence-construction as soon as 'elde' becomes the subject. The second and third lines (1208 – 9) are run-on lines, giving a clear break from the formal couplets of the 'poverte' section. We should also notice that the old wife's – and Alison's – teasing irony is back as she calls her snobbish rapist husband 'ye gentils of honour'. Finally, notice the sudden contrast between the 'poverte' section with its overt refer-ences to 'auctoritee' and paraphrases of classical wisdom, and the offhand dismissal of 'auctoritee', much more characteristic of Ali-son's frame of mind: 'And auctours shal I fynden, as I gesse'.

By the time she begins to offer the knight a choice, colloquial style is fully re-established, and a conversational phrase smoothly completes the line: 'For filthe and eelde, also moot I thee'. The old wife ends her strictures with a change of subject and mood as abrupt as anything in the Prologue:

> But nathelees, syn I knowe youre delit,
> I shal fulfille youre worldly appetit.

The terms 'delit' and 'worldly appetit' complete our return to the world of Alison of Bath, where sexual desire is the most powerful force in nature.

This return of Alison's dramatic presence has a further effect. Irony and cynicism are quickly re-established, and the subject of 'elde' is dismissed. The argument does not have to be convincing because it is entertaining, and it is appropriate that Alison should dismiss 'elde' lightly and quickly, reminding us of the nostalgia for youth she expressed in her Prologue, and her equivocal tone in dismissing the subject then: 'Lat go, farewel! The devel go therwith!'

The choice and the ending (lines 1219–64)

The end of the Tale is comic, and closely resembles the end of Alison's Prologue. The choice offered by the old wife is straightforward. Either she will be 'foul and old' but 'a trewe, humble wyf', or she will be 'yong and fair' but she says it is very likely – 'may wel be' – that she will be unfaithful, and ruin his reputation. This challenge fits into the cynical framework of Alison's outlook on life. She makes the assumption that only an old, ugly woman will be humble and true, with the parallel assumption that promiscuity goes inevitably with youth and beauty. We should also notice that the knight cannot possibly choose. If she remains 'foul and old' he does not want her at all: he showed this by hiding 'as an owle' on his wedding day, and with his subsequent misery in their bridal bed. Her promise to be 'humble' and 'trewe' would intensify his suffering, therefore. On the other hand, he cannot choose her 'yong and fair' because her threat of infidelity hits his most sensitive weakness – his snobbery. Notice that the hag does not attack his heart, to make him jealous, but his 'hous', to make him ashamed. In such circumstances it is impossible for him to choose either option.

He does not respond to the choice immediately, which provides a measure of how much he has matured since he tried to answer the life-question on the spot. We can imagine that he explores the two options and realises that he faces a hopeless choice: he is in her power as neither decision can alter his fate, so he 'sore siketh'. The knight gives his wife 'soveraynetee' after the same unspecified time as Jankyn did: he speaks 'atte laste'. The content of his answer also echoes Jankyn, for he both gives her power and at the same time urges her to use discretion:

> Cheseth yourself which may be moost plesance,
> And moost honour to yow and me also.

This is very like Jankyn's:

> Keep thyn honour, and keep eek myn estaat.

Jankyn and the knight also share a formal, almost legal, diction as they relinquish power, emphasised by the knight's word 'governance' and Jankyn's 'estaat'.

The echoes relating these two scenes continue. The assertive accent on the first syllable with which Alison opens the two lines following Jankyn's submission, '*After* that' and '*God* helpe me so' is emphatically present when the old wife gleefully exclaims '*Kys* me'. She promises to be 'good and trewe' while Alison was 'kynde' and 'also trewe' to Jankyn; and where the old wife becomes as 'fair' as any lady: 'That is bitwixe the est and eke the west', Alison was as 'kynde' 'As any wyf from Denmark unto Ynde.' Chaucer clearly expects us to compare thse two scenes; and the effect is to point up their significant differences. First, the knight's happiness includes sensual delight because the hag has become young and beautiful. This is powerfully expressed by the image of 'a bath of blisse', and Alison dwells on their sexual energy:

> A thousand tyme a-rewe he gan hir kisse,
> And she obeyed hym in every thyng
> That myghte doon hym plesance or likyng.

This element is absent from the reconciliation of Alison and Jankyn. The second point of difference is equally suggestive. While a gentle blessing concluded her Prologue, her Tale finishes on a provocative note: she invokes Christ, and prays him first to send her the means of satisfying her lust – 'housbondes meeke, yonge, and fressh abedde' – then to kill off the men she hates, those:

> That wol nat be governed by hir wyves;
> And olde and angry nygardes of dispence.

The irony of this is most shocking in her use of 'grace' to describe the power to outlive a husband. This recalls the beginning of her Prologue, when she argued that sexuality is a 'yifte' of God's grace, so in wearing out husbands she was doing God's will. The beginning of the text is also recalled by the contrast between good and bad men. With exact irony, Chaucer's Wife reverses her original judgement. She curses the 'goode' rich old men, and longs for 'badde' young men who are 'fressh abedde' like Jankyn. Within this reversal, the hopelessness of her fantasy is betrayed. The young men she married in real life were tyrannous, not 'meeke', and her old husbands were meek, not 'angry'.

These echoes in the Tale's finale are a reminder of Alison's contradictory character. In a magical fantasy world she can create and dwell upon a 'bath of blisse' fulfilling 'worldly appetit'; but we are not allowed to forget that her real life is different and still problematic.

5 THEMES AND ISSUES

5.1 THEMES

Marriage

The theme of marriage announced so resoundingly in the second line presents two issues: first, marriage as an institution, the legal and religious union of two people, is portrayed in the text; and second, emotional and sexual relationships become a complex theme as the Wife describes her 'experience'. Both aspects of the marriage theme have to be treated carefully because Alison's narrative is full of digressions and covert red herrings.

Initially, the debate centres around the institution of marriage, and the Wife argues against the traditional view that it is a holy contract for life, so widows and widowers should remain single. The argument becomes inextricably confused as she uses Solomon (who had many wives at once) to justify 'bigamye' (having several spouses in succession). As we noted, the argument is not really about marriage at all: it is about promiscuity. While Alison marshals references and confuses the issue, Chaucer provides an undercurrent of ironic criticism in her ambiguous references to the scriptures. Two references in particular indicate that we should treat the Wife's 'auctoritees' with scepticism. In one, she compares herself to a vessel of 'tree' in the Lord's household, a reference to II Timothy. Chaucer's audience would recognise the reference and also be aware of its conventional interpretation in the *Glossa*: 'Just as wooden and earthern vessels are of value for cleansing gold and silver vessels, in the same way, the evil are of profit for the improvement of the good' (*Glossa Major*, 114, col. 635). So in claiming to be a useful wooden vessel, the Wife unintentionally defines herself as 'evil', of use only as a foil to the good. In another reference she praises Solomon's polygamy. Again, Chaucer's audience would be familiar with the effect of polygamy on Solomon: 'And when he was now old, his heart was now turned away by women to follow strange gods: and his heart was not perfect with the Lord his God' (3 Kings, 11). Closer examination of all Alison's scriptural references shows further revealing ambiguities. The audience can see that the Wife's pursuit of lust and 'bigamye' is a sinful error, and she stands condemned, ironically, out of her own mouth.

In spite of her distortions, then, scriptural approval of chastity, continence and monogamy are upheld by the subtle irony of the 'auctoritees' referred to. The fourteenth-century institution of marriage is criticised, however. The Prologue as a whole is a strong implicit criticism of the commercial marriages that were common at the time and led to such unequal matches as Alison's first three. She was married at the age of twelve to a 'riche, and olde' man. In other words she was sold to an old man when she was a child, because he coveted her youth and beauty. How can a young girl cope with this situation? Alison coped by accepting marriage as a commercial bargain, realising the financial value of her sex, and charging her husbands for her favours. It is possible to take this child-wedding as the formative experience that confirmed her cynical attitudes and made, her tragically unable to express her gentler feelings. Chaucer enhances our impression of the damage social attitudes to marriage could do when the Wife refers to her mother's advice:

> But as I folwed ay my dames loore,
> As wel of this as of othere thynges moore.

We presume that Alison was brought up to deceit and to grabbing the main chance, so her cynicism was encouraged from an early age.

The second aspect of the marriage-theme, concerned with love relationships, is largely presented through an extended satire on common attitudes to love between men and women, and the powerful cynicism of the Wife herself. However, the text also shows signs of a mutual contract that might lead to a happier conjugal existence. These are later developed in 'The Franklin's Tale', the final contribution to the 'marriage' group.

During the Wife's Prologue we hear the voices of several stock comic figures. Her sample monologues depict herself as the nagging wife; her old husbands; and finally the woman-hating voice of Jankyn. Chaucer makes full use of these opportunities to present the stock prejudices of his time, but the ironic truth about this multiple-voice technique is that the same attitudes and proverbs are often reiterated by different voices in different contexts. Particularly, there are many echoes between Alison's speech reporting her old husbands' chiding, and Jankyn's actual chiding. In the first, for example, she reports:

> Thou seyst that droppyng houses, and eek smoke,
> And chidyng wyves maken men to flee
> Out of hir owene house; . . .

This is later echoed by Jankyn:

> 'Bet is', quod he, 'hye in the roof abyde,
> Than with an angry wyf doun in the hous'.

The Prologue provides many examples of this technique, with the effect that we question who gains from prejudice. The irony points out that in the battle of the sexes, attack is defence and aggression neither wins nor loses. That attack and defence are interchangeable is underlined when Alison glories in the debased character of women:

> I koude pleyne, and yit was in the gilt,
> Or elles often tyme hadde I been spilt.
> Whoso that first to mille comth, first grynt;
> I pleyned first, so was oure werre ystynt.

The degrading popular view of women and marriage, then, is satirised throughout the Prologue. It is also explicitly denounced, giving rise to passages of heartfelt anger. There is genuine frustration in the Wife's tone as she falsely accuses her old husbands of misogyny. The sustained attack on clerks in lines 688–710 is celebrated as a passage prefiguring the present-day women's liberation movement. It is indeed a powerful indictment, gaining much of its force from the bitter accusation: 'Who peyntede the leon, tel me who?' This line cries out against all the sexism and prejudice that stereotypes women. Alison has been 'peyntede' by a male-dominated society; but the tragedy is that she proudly displays the very colours men attribute to her. She says:

> Deceite, wepyng, spynnyng God hath yive
> To wommen kyndely. . .

Finally, there is a hint in 'The Wife of Bath's Prologue and Tale' of a different way to love. The suggestion of gentler and more generous sides to human nature comes when the men submit to female 'maistrye': once in imagination, and twice in actuality. First, the Wife imagines the words she would like her old husbands to say:

> . . . Wyf, go wher thee liste;
> Taak youre disport, I wol nat leve no talys.
> I knowe yow for a trewe wyf, dame Alys.

These lines stand out from the surrounding bitterness for their trusting and affectionate tone, which appears again in both Jankyn's submission (lines 819–21) and the knight's submission in the Tale (lines 1230–35). Both of the actual submissions also hint at a mutual contract, for the wives are adjured to keep 'honour'; and when the knight calls the old hag 'my lady and my love, and wyf so deere', the incongruousness of his words emphasises their loving tone even more sharply.

We cannot build too much on these glimpses of marital harmony, however, and we must remember that there is a cynical comic dimension to each of these extracts. The Wife's contribution to the theme of marriage in *The Canterbury Tales* remains overwhelmingly satirical and bitter. These hints are left to be developed by the Franklin in his later contribution.

Maistrye

'Maistrye' means the dominating, aggressive attitude the Wife cultivates in order to gain 'soveraynetee' over her husbands. As presented by Alison it is a straightforward theme, not yet developing the subtlety it will take on in 'The Clerk's Tale'. Two main points about 'maistrye' emerge from the text we are studying.

First, 'maistrye' is born of the materialistic attitude to relationships that the Wife adopts. She believes that marriage is a battle for property and supremacy. She says: 'Oon of us two moste bowen, doutelees.' She therefore follows her 'dames loore', using deceit and attack at every opportunity to dominate her husbands. 'Maistrye' demands that the best form of defence is attack (lines 379–94), and that she should take advantage of every weakness she can find in her husband by profiting from his desires (lines 409–11) and systematically betraying his faults to the ridicule of the neighbourhood (lines 534–42). The most fully-described incident which illustrates 'maistrye' is the quarrel between Alison and Jankyn. It is the essence of what she means by 'maistrye', that even in this climax of the desperate struggle between them, she has the aggressive determination to use his remorse cynically, tempting him within range for her vengeful blow. After this she boasts of having 'geten unto me, by maistrie, al the soveraynetee'. 'Maistrye', then, means the determination to battle on without respite until the fight is won. No pity or consideration, nor any form of weakness, can be shown during the battle.

This observation leads to the second point about 'maistrye'. Although Alison is a sturdy woman, there is no suggestion that she is physically stronger than Jankyn. His one blow knocks her out and deafens her for life. In this case, how can 'maistrye' bring her victory? The answer to this is given in different parts of the Prologue and Tale, but nowhere more clearly than in these lines:

> Suffreth alwey, syn ye so wel kan preche;
> And but ye do, certein we shal you teche
> That it is fair to have a wyf in pees.

Here, Alison explains that her husband will experience no 'pees' until he is willing to suffer in 'pacience', or in other words, until he submits to her will. The strength and success of 'maistrye', then, lies in her indomitable will. It therefore presents Jankyn with a choice as impossible as that the old hag offers to her knight in the Tale: a choice between unending strife and misery, and utter submission. The old hag's choice should be seen as the final manifestation of 'maistrye', offering a choice which can be summarised as: death (it does not matter whose!) or surrender.

Gentillesse

Since the idea of 'gentillesse' plays no part in the Wife's Prologue and Tale except in the old wife's speech, there is no need for a summary of this theme: it is adequately discussed in the general commentary. The present discussion focuses on how the old wife's introduction of this theme complicates the total effect of the Tale.

The old wife develops the view that 'gentillesse' is a virtue that anyone may show, rather than an inherited quality. In doing so she describes people who are:

> . . . moost vertuous alway,
> Pryvee and apert, and moost entendeth ay
> To do the gentil dedes that he kan.

And she talks of noble ancestors with their 'vertuous lyvyng'. This emphasis on virtue is in sharp contrast to Alison's practice and her avowed philosophy. It is the antithesis of her incontinent promiscuity and the unchristian, remorseless self-interest she calls 'maistrye'. The introduction of 'gentillesse', then, presents a contradiction in the Wife's overall statement that would seem to make no sense at all. A suggested explanation of this problem appears in the discussion of Alison's character, in the next chapter. For the moment we must accept that the two themes, 'maistrye' and 'gentillesse', represent irreconcilably opposed ideas.

The Wife does not attempt to define the 'vertuous lyvyng' to which she refers. If we judge from her misuse of the Bible and the life she has lived, she would not know how to define it. However, later tales explore the relationships between maistrye, lordship and gentillesse in subtle detail, and therefore reflect more light on the Wife's anomaly than she herself could cast.

5.2 THE TALE AS AN EXEMPLUM

An 'exemplum' is a story used to support a speaker's opinion or moral. The Wife's main thesis is that women should have 'soveraynetee' in marriage because they will then be happy, faithful, and will make their husbands happy. We can look at the Tale to see how well it supports this opinion.

First we must acknowledge that the Wife's argument is manifestly absurd: no Tale could prove to our satisfaction such a partisan idea as universal female 'soveraynetee'. Her overall argument has to be seen in context: it is for Chaucer's use in revealing the Wife's character; and it is an ironic comment on the absurdity of the conventional view that men should always be in charge. Having said this, we can examine the relationship between Tale and Prologue.

Most of the Tale supports the view that women 'moost desiren' 'soveraynetee'. This is reminiscent of the Prologue, where we are more struck by the Wife's overwhelming need for power than persuaded that she ought to have it. The case for women's 'soveraynetee', in both the Prologue and the Tale, rests on Alison's assertion that it is the only way to find happiness in marriage. This in turn rests on the assertion that she was happy with Jankyn, and the ultimate bliss of the knight and the hag in her Tale. On both these occasions, however, Alison only sketches happiness after dwelling on misery. The assertion of perfect happiness is also undermined in the Prologue by the unresolved question of unequal age that has already been discussed. In the Tale, their inequality of age disappears, but the story is weakened as an 'exemplum' by using magic to resolve this central problem. After all, Alison herself could not grow young again, and she began her Tale by reminding the pilgrims that magic does not happen any more, thanks to the Friars!

During the Tale, Alison spends some time convincing her audience that 'soveraynetee' is what women most desire. In the course of developing this argument she lists and dismisses a range of possible answers that are inferior to the 'right' one. People told the knight that women desire 'richesse' or 'honour', 'lust abedde' or 'oftetyme to be wydwe and wedde'. Alison then spends some time on two of the possible answers, one which she considers close to the truth and one on which she casts scorn. It is true, she says, that women love flattery; but it is nonsense to say they love to be thought trustworthy. The development of ideas in this part of the Tale is consistent and convincingly argued, but we should notice that the argument is limited rigidly to the same cynical attitude as prevails in the Prologue. Ideals such as 'love' and 'honour' are ignored or quickly dismissed; the vice of 'flaterye' is encouraged while the quality of trust is scorned. The Tale suits the Prologue by setting the terms of debate rigidly within the bounds of Alison's avowed cynicism about people and life.

The sermon about 'gentillesse' breaks out of this cynical mould, bringing its contrary idea of 'gentil' people dedicated to 'vertuous lyvyng'. However, this again is appropriate to the Prologue, representing the other side of Alison's personality. Like the hidden self which breaks through her surface cynicism in the Prologue, the side of her that believes in equality and 'gentillesse' looks for something higher and better than the temporal world she has to adjust to under the tutelage of her mentor, 'experience'.

'The Wife of Bath's Tale', then, is a very carefully constructed exemplum. It does not support or prove the idea of women's 'soveraynetee', any more than the Prologue succeeds in doing this. Its weaknesses as an exemplum for Alison's purpose, are the magically resolved problem of age, and a belief in higher and better values that cannot be fully repressed. It is a perfect Tale for Chaucer's purpose, however, for it ironically displays the same contradictions and problems that have upset the Wife's peace of mind in her Prologue and in her own life.

6 TECHNICAL FEATURES

6.1 THE WIFE'S CHARACTER

Chaucer's characterisation of Alison of Bath far outstrips any sources or stereotyped figures, and she is developed far beyond medieval literary conventions. The use of a distinctive 'voice' and colloquial language to create her unique personality, and the complexity of her character as digressions and inconsistencies reveal an inner self, all show that Chaucer was breaking new literary ground with his creation. This discussion looks at the interweaving of medieval and modern forms of understanding through the figure of Alison, by which means Chaucer uses her character to depict the full complexity of his times. We can distinguish two sides to the Wife's character.

The image she projects for her audience is of a confident, aggressive woman, cruel to her husbands and insensitive. She boasts that she wore her husbands out, and 'I laughe whan I thynke' of this; that she scolded them 'whan that for syk unnethes myghte they stonde'. She remains combative to the end, not softening even when Jankyn relents, and she is careful not to betray any need for love. When she tells of dreaming about Jankyn, for example, she quickly explains: 'And al was fals; I dremed of it right naught'. As we found in the commentary, Alison's image of herself is utterly cynical. Marriages – at least, her first three marriages – are a commercial venture, love is lust, and other emotions such as affection or tolerance are weaknesses.

There are cracks in this façade, however, and a different aspect of the Wife appears if we look through these cracks to the inner self she unwittingly betrays. This different side of her character shows her as vulnerable and needing true affection, using 'maistrye' and deceit as a defence against male domination. She longs to be trusted, hoping her husbands will say 'I knowe you for a trewe wyf, dame Alys'; she is angered by their suspicion, but most of all she is hurt both by her fourth husband's unfaithfulness, and by Jankyn's cruel prejudice, suffering in a way she finds difficult to describe:

Who wolde wene, or who wolde suppose,
The wo that in myn herte was, and pyne?

She is nostalgic for youth, expresses sadness about becoming old, and reveals that she longed for Jankyn who had 'enchanted' her. Finally, she is 'as kynde as any wyf from Denmark unto Ynde, and also trewe', when Jankyn finally submits. This softer side of her character only breaks out into action at one time in her life: when she gives all her property to Jankyn and allows herself to be beaten and charmed at the beginning of her fifth marriage.

These two sides of the Wife's personality are contradictory. Our task, therefore, is to understand this paradox by examining how Chaucer has created her as a complete but self-contradictory character. We can begin by looking at the medieval explanation of her problematic nature: her horoscope. Alison explains that she was born under the contrary influences of Venus and Mars, and identifies the two planets with the two sides of her nature. She says 'I am al Venerien in feelynge' but 'myn herte is Marcien'. Venus gave her 'lust' and 'likerousnesse' and Mars provided her 'sturdy hardynesse'. She goes further in identifying marks on her body and her features with the two planets, and bemoans her fate in being born subject to such incompatible influences: 'Allas! allas! that evere love was synne!' The astrological explanation of her character absolves her of responsibility: all she has done in life, including her frankly admitted promiscuity, is the inevitable result of a malignant combination of planets:

I folwed ay myn inclinacioun
By vertu of my constellacioun.

Nowadays we are likely to take astrology with a pinch of salt: it is amusing to read your 'stars' in the newspaper, but nothing more, but the student of Chaucer must remember that astrology was a respected 'science' in the fourteenth century, and was applied to practical purposes such as medical diagnosis and treatment. The following selection of extracts from astrologers describing the characters of those born under Venus and Mars should provide enough startling reminders of the Wife of Bath, to show that Chaucer meant Alison's horoscope to be a credible explanation of what she is like. These astrologers are all quoted in Walter Clyde Curry's 'The Wife of

Bath', which appears in *Chaucer: Modern Essays in Criticism* (see Further Reading).

The woman born when Taurus is in the ascendant, for example, is 'florid of complexion', and she 'shall be lightly given to affairs of the heart'; 'She shall be inconstant, changeable, speaking (or gossiping) with fluency and volubility, now to this one now to that'. The beautiful nature ascribed to women born under Venus tells us about Alison's 'inner' character. The Venusian woman is 'gentle in disposition', 'passionate and voluptuous by nature but religious and righteous'. 'They drink much and eat little; they have a good digestion, which provokes passion and an ardent desire for coition – but they are noble in life and cleanly in act', then 'they delight in feminine ornaments and are given to adorning their bodies in elegant and smart attire . . . they are tender by nature and prone to shed tears'. In this portrait of the Venusian woman we can see the Wife's 'likerousnesse', her love of wine and its link with passion, and the soft heart she so briefly reveals: but all are tempered by a gentleness and righteousness lacking in Alison. The same astrologer writes that Venusian women are 'Temperamental by nature, they show displeasure easily and indulge in complaints, employ crafty devices, and refresh themselves by a return to peace and affection'. Another astrologer sees deeper faults, writing that they are 'volatile, capricious, and inconstant, especially when they are not maintained sumptuously and in grand style', and even more startlingly concludes that 'Their amorous actions bring it about that, while they serve themselves by deceptions and cajoleries, they are pleasing and attractive at the same time, forcing the fascinated will of the lover to surrender'. Venus, then, has several propensities in common with Alison of Bath.

Astrologers all agree on the evil influence of Mars. Their descriptions are so derogatory that a few choice words will convey their tone satisfactorily. Mars 'Changes all these prognostications (Venusian virtues) into vain words and lies'. People influenced by Mars are 'greedy and rapacious, rash, reckless, criminal, rejoicing in causing unhappiness', or the 'native shall be voluptuous and a fornicator . . . becoming guilty of incest, or committing adultery'. Mars, in short, takes away nobility and righteousness and adds insatiable lusts for fornication and money, and unscrupulous abuse of other people. It is clear that the materialism and cynical opportunism of the Wife is something she has unfortunately been given by Mars.

Further reading of astrologers and physiognomists of Chaucer's time shows that even the Wife's physical appearance, as described in 'The General Prologue', is modelled closely on her horoscope. We should, then, take account of Alison's horoscope when we study her character. The medieval view suggests that she is tragic: the hopeless product of contrary stars, doomed both to follow the wicked battling ways of Mars, and painfully possessed of a soft sensitivity from Venus that makes her morbidly desire the bliss she cannot achieve.

A modern view of Alison's character also exists, however, explaining her significance in different terms. A modern approach to character uses psychological and social terms. A psychological reading of Alison tells us that she projects a raucous image of herself as cynical and unshockable. She represses her gentler nature because she is scared of revealing her vulnerable inner self. She avoids and delays telling of the weakest moments in her life, for example by digressing before revealing her feelings about her fourth husband's unfaithfulness, or before telling the pilgrims what happened when she walked in the fields with Jankyn. In psychological terms, the soft inner nature that craves love and trust is repressed, and she shields herself from male domination behind a comic and provocative self-image.

This interpretation is interesting as it leads us to notice further subtleties in Chaucer's construction of the Prologue and Tale. First, there is the long diatribe against women that Alison puts into the mouths of her first three husbands. We know that they were meek and subservient men, and she scolded them. Yet in her scolding Alison imagines a husband who is strong and fights to dominate her. It is reasonable to speculate that she unconsciously longed for a stronger, dominant man while she was married to these old weaklings, and used her scoldings to imagine such a man. Eventually, of course, she falls in love with the intolerant Jankyn, and is temporarily subdued by him.

Second, when Alison finally chooses Jankyn 'for love, and no richesse', she makes light of the difference in their ages, saying that she was a young forty:

> As help me God! I was a lusty oon,
> And faire, and riche, and yong, and wel bigon.

Chaucer treats this problem with the most delicate subtlety, but the inclusion of 'riche' in this list of her attractions betrays Alison's attempt to deceive herself. Her age could not be ignored, and there was some fear in living with her twenty-year-old husband at the time when her own beauty was fast fading. That she did fade we also know from her own mouth when she says 'The flour is goon . . . . The bren, as I best kan, now moste I selle'.

Age, then, is a problem Alison cannot overcome. With delicate psychological insight Chaucer passes on to the Tale, where Alison uses magic to solve in fantasy the intractable problem of growing old. Eventually she is able to indulge her own wish-fulfilment fantasy of eager intercourse between equals: 'A thousand tyme a-rewe he gan hir kisse'.

Finally we come to the question of the hag's sermon on 'gentillesse'. Many critics have remarked that the moral emphasis on 'vertu' found in this speech is uncharacteristic of the Wife, and there is a brief discussion of this point in the commentary. Can the modern view of Alison's character throw light on this anomaly? Perhaps the sermon on 'gentillesse' is not out of character, but ironically true to Alison's inner self. She cannot abandon her cynical defence while speaking for herself, so the theme of 'gentillesse' has no place in her Prologue; but Alison does express the other side of her nature through the hag in her Tale. The attitude to 'gentillesse' she reveals is also, suitably, a modern, egalitarian point of view.

To complement this reading of Alison's character, a modern analysis sees people as the product of their society: their upbringing and experiences mould them and affect their personalities. Taking a 'social' view of the Wife, she was brought up to look at marriage as a commercial bargain, and was sold off to a repulsive old man at the age of twelve. The influence of this background would naturally inspire her to react by building up an aggressive shell, and would reinforce the cynical commercialism she had already been taught.

To sum up, we can see her as a tragic figure caught between the contrary planetary influences of Venus and Mars; or she is a vulnerable girl who was thrown into life too young by a cynical society. Her inner feelings could only be expresssed accidentally, so she developed an abrasive exterior and repressed her need for love. In this view she is also tragic because she never finds happiness in equality, and can only allow herself the luxury of falling in love when she is already growing old. The misery of her wasted youth is added to her other regrets.

Chaucer's genius is in weaving together the different strands of his times and creating the Wife as a character who is of all time, as significant for us in the twentieth century as she was for the medieval world. Her significance is ultimately in the tragedy of her wasted life, which we may see as the result of rough experience on a certain kind of nature; but which the medieval world would see as the tragic result of her error in valuing the temporal world above the spiritual world and perverting the gospel, thanks to her particularly ill-fated nativity. It is our task as students of Chaucer to realise that both explanations have equal validity. Both emphasise the bitterness of her life and the inevitable tragedy of her moral error.

6.2 STYLE AND IMAGERY

Verse and diction

The text is composed in iambic pentameter, which means that each line is made up of five two-syllable feet with stress on the second syllable (an iambic foot sounds like 'de-dum'). The opening line of the Prologue is regular:

Expérieńce, though nóon auctóriteé

Chaucer's pentameters are also largely rhyming couplets, although he does occasionally use alternating rhymes or rhyme three lines together. So the form of 'The Wife of Bath's Prologue and Tale' is regular and strict, and it is due to Chaucer's brilliance as a poet that it never seems false or becomes monotonous, but is natural, volatile, and exciting throughout.

Chaucer is a master of variations in speed and tone. Often the rhythms of natural speech override the iambic pattern, and irregular lines portray sudden emotion. For example, Alison's exclamation after Jankyn knocks her down begins emphatically with her cry 'O!', reversing the first foot of the line:

'Ó! hastow sláyn me, fálse theéf?' I seýde

The poet often does this to express outrage or surprise, but a more subtle use of this effect occurs when the sudden change of tone portrays Alison pulling herself together after a digression, as for example when she dismisses her reflections about youth and age, and the first two feet of the line are emphatically reversed:

Lát go, fárewel! the dével gó therwith!

Another common effect occurs when two stressed syllables are put next to each other. This has an emphatic effect and slows the pace of the verse, so the outrageous daring of Alison's action when she tears Jankyn's book 'halts' the verse in this way:

> Al sodeynly thre léves have I plyght
> Out of his book, right as he radde, and eke . . .

Notice that the rhythm of the second line here is very irregular and broken, conveying Alison's anger and fear when she realised what she had done.

Chaucer also phrases his verse to achieve variety of pace. From the excitement of the line just quoted, which is twice broken by punctuation, Chaucer moves easily on to uninterrupted speed in the next two lines of rapid action as Alison knocks Jankyn down. Two run-on lines in succession give this rushing effect:

> and eke
> I with my fest so took hym on the cheke
> That in oure fyr he fil bakward adoun.

The vivid variety of Chaucer's verse matches an unpredictable diction that is the hallmark of Alison's speech. She is portrayed as an eclectic in her use of language: five different husbands and wide travel gave her ample opportunities to absorb different styles of language, and they all form an exciting mixture when she speaks. Three particular characteristics of her language stand out.

First, she uses common domestic words and phrases, such as 'bren', 'rafte', 'barly-breed', a vessel of 'tree', and her energy she calls 'pith'. These short, earthy words give a sense that she is in constant contact with basic natural processes, living a life of appetite and sensation rather like the domestic and farm animals to which she constantly compares herself. In keeping with this language Alison has a powerful command of homely wisdom, and recites her stock of sayings fluently:

> Ne noon so grey goos gooth ther in the lake
> As, sëistow, wol been withoute make.

The finest phrases in this style, however, are her vivid and original descriptions of feeling. She has a knack of using the imagery of common life in a way that immediately conveys sensations, in lines like:

> It tikleth me aboute myn herte roote

or

> That in his owene grece I made hym frye

The second distinctive style Chaucer weaves into her voice is her rich fund of innuendo, that contrasts hilariously with her earthy frankness. For example, she admits that she cannot keep 'my chambre of Venus from a good felawe'. A man is called plainly a 'good felawe', but instead of a plain word for her genitals she uses the elaborate and rather coy phrase 'chambre of Venus'. Elsewhere, she twice refers to her vagina as her 'bele chose' in mock-courtly French, and once as her 'quoniam' in mock-Latin. These examples show that she has a lively ability to play on words for comic effect, a point that is underlined by her puns on 'licence' and 'lymytacioun', which raise laughter at the Friar's expense. A more ambiguous use of courtly and euphemistic diction occurs, however, when she cannot bring herself to speak openly of her fourth husband's mistress. A wealth of jealousy and insecurity is expressed when Alison dignifies her hated rival with the precious romance term 'paramour'.

Finally Chaucer adds a liberal portion of academic words and phrases to this riot of language. We assume that Alison's scholarship was absorbed from her fifth husband, and the poet uses her learned style to build up another contrast with her earthy frankness. Lines 115–62 provide many examples of this technique. The high-flown pomposity of phrases such as 'membres . . . of generacion' and 'purgacioun of uryne' or the words 'instrument' and 'engendrure', sit comically alongside earthy language like 'bothe thynges smale', 'harneys', the euphemism 'refresshed', and the frankness with which Alison says that people with genitals do not have to 'goon and usen hem', or declares roundly that her husband will 'have it bothe eve and morwe'.

The old wife's speech in the Tale demonstrates a greater reliance on learned style, deploying words and constructions as would a scholar. Words like 'temporel', 'strange' and 'office natureel' appear in their philosophical sense in formal constructions:

> For of oure eldres may we no thyng clayme
> But temporel thyng, that man may hurte and mayme.

In this speech there is much use of reasoning conjunctions such as 'for', 'thanne', 'yet' and 'therefore'; we claim our gentillesse 'of' (not 'from') our ancestors, and verb–subject inversions abound: 'that deed is', 'be he', 'gentil men ycalled be', and many more. This speech with its particularly scholastic style is discussed in the general commentary; the rest of the Prologue and Tale, however, is a testament to the sheer variety of language at Chaucer's call.

Imagery

Alison uses two distinct kinds of imagery to describe herself and her relationships. First, there is the constant undercurrent of animal and domestic metaphors, when, for example, she is stubborn 'as a leonesse' with Jankyn, or knew how to 'byte and whyne' like 'an hors'. Many more examples are pointed out in the general commentary, but we should also notice that the same kind of imagery provides her with happier pictures, comparing herself when younger with birds. She remembers being 'joly as a pye' when she could 'synge . . . as any nyghtyngale'. These images express Alison's instinctive sensuality, then, but have a more complex effect as well. First, they emphasise her openly degrading view of herself, her admission that she is a vulgar creature living a low, animal life. At the same time, lighter natural images convey a desire for freedom, and intense enjoyment of being alive.

The second strand of images is made up of goods and chattels, the imagery of the market-place. Alison presents herself as an object for sale and this metaphor runs throughout the Prologue. Her adage is: 'Wynne whoso may, for al is for to selle' and she suggests that she could sell her 'bele chose', and that women are 'bacyns, lavours, . . . spoones and stooles, and al swich housbondrye' that men 'bye'. The majority of these comparisons refer to objects of little value, giving the same effect of self-denigration as we notice in her more vulgar animal imagery. Chaucer's use of gold as an image of preciousness complicates the situation, however. A chaste saint is a vessel of 'gold', in contrast to Alison, at the beginning of the Prologue. This is a reference to St Paul, but Chaucer shows how Alison's failure to distinguish spiritual from physical beauty confuses her later in the Prologue, when she describes the page Jankyn's beautiful hair 'shynynge as gold so fyn'. Eventually, desire, passion and preciousness come together boldly when she explains her dream to Jankyn: 'blood bitokeneth gold, as me was taught'. These images show Alison's failure to recognise a separate spiritual value; but only in the fantasy of her Tale can Alison entirely forget the base images of herself that dominate the rest of the text. At the end of the Tale the old wife is transformed into a beautiful woman and is described in imagery suggesting power, luxury and riches as well:

> as fair to seene
> As any lady, emperice, or queene

In addition to the two major motifs we have discussed, there are plentiful incidental metaphors and similes. One noticeable example is the comparison Alison uses in replying to the Pardoner. Her life-experience, she suggests, is like a barrel of ale: at first it tastes fresh, but as you drink more of it the taste becomes increasingly sour. This comparison stands on its own, expressing subtly and in its own different context, the bitter regret that Alison felt at becoming old.

6.3 DRAMATIC DEVICES

In 'The Wife of Bath's Prologue and Tale' Chaucer uses every means at his disposal to dramatise, so the reader can be forgiven for feeling like the audience at a play rather than a reader of a long monologue.

The most pervasive dramatic device is the one common to all of *The Canterbury Tales*: the audience of pilgrims we come to know so intimately as individuals. Chaucer never allows this dramatic context to leave our sight. For example, Alison is interrupted twice, first by the Pardoner and then by the Friar and the Summoner. The interruptions perform two functions. First, they remind us of the framework, advancing the story of the pilgrimage by developing the characters of those involved. Second, they provide us with a dramatic measure of Alison's personality. She is full of confidence and in control of her audience when she rebuffs the Pardoner, for the cracks in her confident self-image have not as yet begun to appear. When the Friar interrupts, however, she is weaker, unable to take control for a critical moment before the Host intervenes to restore order. Chaucer uses this drama to show us how far self-revelation and indulgence of nostalgia have distracted Alison's defences during her Prologue.

It would be short-sighted to suggest that the interruptions are the only reminders of the audience, however. The truth is that they are seldom far from our minds, and Chaucer's genius is to play upon the dramatic situation, bringing now this, now that pilgrim into our minds as Alison's narrative unfolds, reviving what we already know about them and foreshadowing points about them that will be revealed later in the whole work. For example, the portrait of the rich old husbands will come back to the reader's mind when the Merchant regrets his marriage and tells his tale of January and May. What must be his feelings as Alison revels in their sufferings? We know that the Friar must be squirming as he hears Alison digress about him and his brothers, but what of her angry attack on the clerks: how did the Clerk respond? Finally, as the old wife discusses inherited 'gentillesse', how sadly does the Franklin shake his head, thinking of the son who is such a clot that no amount of schooling and good company can turn him into a gentleman? These speculations show how vividly we are kept aware of the effect of the Tales on their audience, by the poet's technique of having one pilgrim either innocently or deliberately touch on the sensitivities of the others.

Alison's speaking style also keeps us constantly in touch with the dramatic situation. There is a detailed discussion of her skill as a comic raconteur at the beginning of the general commentary, showing how she uses variations of style and speed and careful timing to deliver her jokes with maximum effectiveness. Finally, she speaks directly to the pilgrims several times. She tells them where they are in the story:

> Now wol I speken of my fourthe housbonde

and

> Now wol I tellen forth what happed me.

She loses her thread and chats to them while she collects her wits:

> But now, sire, lat me se, what I shal seyn?

She asks their permission to tell them the story of Midas:

> Witnesse on Myda, – wol ye heere the tale?

Chaucer uses all these dramatic devices to keep us involved in the dramatic context, and the effect is to add layers of irony to the narrative by bringing to our notice the many different attitudes of her listeners.

There is also intensive dramatisation within the Prologue and Tale. There are frequent quotations from the Bible and other authors, and digressions alternate with narrative throughout the Prologue. Most tellingly, Chaucer makes his raconteur use direct and reported speech extensively, so we are treated to long speeches from Alison to her old husbands, from them to her, from Jankyn, and from the old wife in the Tale. The obvious effect of this device is to break up the monotony of a long recital. Chaucer uses the technique thoroughly to this end, providing racy colloquial dialogue for the knight and the old wife, for example, or satirising Alison's aggressive nagging and Jankyn's pedantic tone, so ensuring a variety of voices in the text. However, a more important effect of this 'multiple-voice' technique is structural. Layer upon layer of dramatic irony is built into the narrative, and Chaucer fully exploits the consequent interplay of cross-references and attitudes. This device intensifies humour, reveals the ambiguities of Alison's feelings, and plays shifting lights on the major themes of marriage and sexual attitudes. How complex the whole dramatic structure is can be demonstrated by trying to describe the circumstances of one speech. Chaucer tells us what Alison told the pilgrims that she had persuaded her husbands they said to her when they were drunk; he then tells us, however, that Alison confided to the pilgrims that she made it all up herself! We have to make a careful and thoughtful choice in deciding what to believe when reading such a complex and ironic text.

7 SPECIMEN PASSAGE

AND

CRITICAL COMMENTARY

7.1 SPECIMEN PASSAGE

The Wife of Bath's Prologue, (lines 543–99)

And so bifel that ones in a Lente –
So often tymes I to my gossyb wente,
For evere yet I loved to be gay,
And for to walke in March, Averill, and May,
Fro hous to hous, to heere sondry talys –
That Jankyn clerk, and my gossyb dame Alys,
And I myself, into the feeldes wente.
Myn housbonde was at Londoun al that Lente;
I hadde the bettre leyser for to pleye,
And for to se, and eek for to be seye
Of lusty folk. What wiste I wher my grace
Was shapen for to be, or in what place?
Therfore I made my visitaciouns
To vigilies and to processiouns,
To prechyng eek, and to thise pilgrimages,
To pleyes of myracles, and to mariages,
And wered upon my gaye scarlet gytes.
Thise wormes, ne thise motthes, ne thise mytes,
Upon my peril, frete hem never a deel;
And wostow why? for they were used weel.
    Now wol I tellen forth what happed me.
I seye that in the feeldes walked we,
Til trewely we hadde swich daliance,
This clerk and I, that of my purveiance
I spak to hym and seyde hym how that he,

If I were wydwe, sholde wedde me.
For certeinly, I sey for no bobance,
Yet was I nevere withouten purveiance
Of mariage, n'of othere thynges eek.
I holde a mouses herte nat worth a leek
That hath but oon hole for to sterte to,
And if that faille, thanne is al ydo.
    I bar hym on honde he hadde enchanted me, –
My dame taughte me that soutiltee.
And eek I seyde I mette of hym al nyght,
He wolde han slayn me as I lay upright,
And al my bed was ful of verray blood;
But yet I hope that he shal do me good,
For blood bitokeneth gold, as me was taught.
And al was fals; I dremed of it right naught,
But as I folwed ay my dames loore,
As wel of this as of othere thynges moore.
    But now, sire, lat me se, what I shal seyn?
A ha! by God, I have my tale ageyn.
    Whan that my fourthe housbonde was on beere,
I weep algate, and made sory cheere,
As wyves mooten, for it is usage,
And with my coverchief covered my visage,
But for that I was purveyed of a make,
I wepte but smal, and that I undertake.
    To chirche was myn housonde born a-morwe
With neighebores, that for hym maden sorwe;
And Jankyn, oure clerk, was oon of tho.
As help me God! whan that I saugh hym go
After the beere, me thoughte he hadde a paire
Of legges and of feet so clene and faire
That al myn herte I yaf unto his hoold.

7.2 CRITICAL COMMENTARY

We have looked at this passage in the general commentary. Alison
has reached the point in her narrative where she is telling the pilgrims
about her courtship with Jankyn, and we know that the story
advances in bits and pieces interspersed with digressions. Now we
want to look at the poetry in detail to see how the technique creates
Alison's dramatic presence and helps to reveal her complex
character.

The Prologue is written in iambic couplets, and in the passage we are looking at the metre is regular throughout. In spite of this we read with an impression of variety of pace: the regular form does not engender monotony. This is because Chaucer controls the pace of his verse according to a larger rhythmic scheme that works differently from the regular metrical numbers. We can detect these broader rhythms by analysing the punctuation. In this passage there is a wave-like rhythm that suits the growing and receding waves of reminiscence and emotion that repeatedly flow over Alison as she tells her story. The first seven lines make a good example of what I might call a 'wave' digression:

> And so bifel that ones in a Lente –
> So often tymes I to my gossyb wente,
> For evere yet I loved to be gay,
> And for to walke in March, Averill, and May,
> Fro hous to hous, to heere sondry talys –
> That Jankyn clerk, and my gossyb dame Alys,
> And I myself, into the feeldes wente.

The opening couplet is broken in half by the dash that introduces a digression, and the main middle part of the sentence is a long loop away from the narrative. We return to the story abruptly after 'talys', although we still have to wait for the final four words – 'into the feeldes wente' – before Alison gives us the main clause. It is a sentence designed for suspense, and the whole loop of rambling reminiscence (lines 544–47) is contained within that suspense. In addition, the four lines of digression are punctuated by commas that increase in frequency to a climax of short phrases 'March, Averill, and May, fro hous to hous, to heere sondry talys – ' that leads in turn to a sudden break, bringing us back to the narrative with a bump. This is the structure I have compared to a wave: it swells and quickens, then suddenly breaks and recedes. Looking at the punctuation can show clearly how Chaucer creates the rhythms we sense as we read. You can see a similar effect in these lines:

> Therfore I made my visitaciouns
> To vigilies and to processiouns,
> To prechyng eek, and to thise pilgrimages,
> To pleyes of myracles, and to mariages.

In this case the dreamlike quality of Alison's memories is enhanced by polysyllabic rhyme-words and elaborate two-syllable rhymes, 'visitaciouns/processiouns' and 'pilgrimages/mariages', that add a chanting tone to the lines. There are further examples in the passage (see lines 577–81 and 587–92), and these waves in the poetry create the washes of emotion that flow through Alison as she tells about this poignant time in her life.

There is tension in the passage also, however, for Alison does not give in to her emotive memories without a struggle. In contrast to the rhythms analysed above, there are flat, brief statements that carry the narrative forward, and seem to be isolated from their surroundings. For example, we are told:

> Myn housbonde was at Londoun al that Lente;

and Alison adopts a matter-of-fact tone when she returns to her story at:

> Whan that my fourthe housbonde was on beere.

These are like reference points in the story, anchored bits of fact in Alison's flow of self-revelation. They also seem dull and restrained in contrast to the rest, and their isolation suggests they are part of her effort to restrain and control herself.

The tense, alternating rhythms I have described continue through the passage, until finally she loses all restraint and rushes unchecked through two-and-a-half lines:

> . . . me thoughte he hadde a paire
> Of legges and of feet so clene and faire
> That al myn herte I yaf unto his hoold.

Perhaps this final outpouring of words simply suits the punch-line to her joke; but we can suggest that it also denotes the moment when her battle for self-control is over. She has finally found a way to express her love for Jankyn in the safe form of a cynical joke, there is no more need for restraint, and Chaucer conveys her relief in the gathering rush of these lines.

Looking at the rhythms of this passage provides one other outstanding moment. See how Chaucer chops the phrases into small units when Alison forgets her place and stops to find her way back to the story:

> But now, sire, lat me se, what I shal seyn?
> A ha! by God, I have my tale ageyn.

Chaucer's mastery of colloquial exclamation reveals Alison's state of mind. She was truly daydreaming of those walks in the fields with Jankyn. The return to the present is choppy and disturbing, and there is psychological justness in the fact that her next thought (perhaps prompted by suddenly remembering that she is a widow again) is of death. Some of the ideas about Alison's feelings that I have found from analysing the rhythm may seem over-speculative; but you can see how richly the poetry suggests her living experience as she talks.

Chaucer's poetry always shows a lot of alliteration, and this passage is no exception. The alliteration is often incidental, merely contributing to the 'music' of the language like 'prechyng . . . pilgrimages . . . pleyes' or 'myracles . . . mariages' in the passage. Sometimes, however, it has a more purposeful effect. In this passage we can hear Alison's disgust in the heavy 'th' and 'm' sounds of: 'Thise wormes, ne thise motthes, ne thise mytes'. One other example is quite extraordinary in its effect. There is a leaden, final tone as Alison tells us that her husband was 'at Londoun al that Lente'. The two capitalised words have a deadening sound. It is difficult to describe the effect of the third alliterated word 'leyser', in the next line, however. 'Leyser' has a rising, lingering sound expressing Alison's change of mood as she begins another reminiscence. That the same alliteration can express such contrary moods and yet link them together, is a testament to the astonishing skill with which Chaucer orchestrated his verse.

Finally, notice the lively realism of Alison's speech. Her presence becomes immediate as she loses her thread and finds it again; as she asks an arch rhetorical question with a wicked play on the word 'grace';

> . . . What wiste I wher my grace
> Was shapen for to be, or in what place?

as she fills in a line casually:

> For certeinly, I sey for no bobance,

and in her exclamation when the final joke occurs:

> As help me God!

A close look at the texture of Chaucer's writing is immensely rewarding. In this passage we can see with what subtly fine technique the poet creates the voluble and volatile presence of Alison of Bath, at the same time dramatically revealing the conflicts within her character.

8 SOME CRITICAL
VIEWS

It is important to remember that reading critical works is only a
secondary activity for students of literature: there is no substitute for
close, thoughtful study of the text itself. However, a text as provocative as 'The Wife of Bath's Prologue and Tale' throws up controversies
we should be aware of, both because they can stimulate our thinking
about the text, and because they often find their way into examination questions. This survey is only intended to point out the main
areas of controversy.

The Wife's character

Most critics agree that Chaucer was indebted to a tradition of comic
figures and to La Vieille from Jean de Meun's *Roman de la Rose*, in
creating the Wife. Most agree that he went far beyond his sources.
Charles Muscatine, for example, (*Chaucer and the French Tradition*,
California and London, 1966) writes of Chaucer's 'naturalization' of
the Wife from many sources to give her 'a lifelike individuality'
creating 'the embodiment of practical experience, of domestic freedom, and of sensuality'. W. C. Curry (in *Chaucer: Modern Essays in
Criticism*, see Further Reading) points out that we should understand
her horoscope, because this 'would seem to be necessary for a
thorough understanding of the poet's original conception'; but he
concludes that she is more than a mere horoscope: 'Under the spell of
Chaucer's pen one rests under the illusion that the Wife of Bath is a
complex human being'.
    The main disagreements between the critics come between those
who emphasise medieval order and see Chaucer as writing with an
over-riding moral purpose, and those who emphasise realism and

humanity. For the former view, D. W. Robertson states that: 'Alisoun of Bath is not a "character" in the modern sense at all, but an elaborate iconographic figure designed to show the manifold implications of an attitude. . . Those who grow sentimental over her "human" qualities are, from a fourteenth-century point of view, simply being misled.' The assumption of such criticism is that Chaucer had no wish to create 'real' individuals and his main purpose was to teach. The second group of critics see Alison as full of positive human qualities. To Maurice Hussey (*Chaucer's World*, London and New York, 1967) she is a figure of 'shameless vitality', and John Speirs remarks that: 'In her own inordinate way she represents life boldly asserted against oppressive forms of death.'

Many find her complex and contradictory. Nevill Coghill writes that she 'contains contradictions', and elaborates: 'This woman is driven by two contrary hungers, for love and for power, and that is the secret of her restlessness. When she has power it is no love, and when she achieves love, her power is gone.' (*The Poet Chaucer*, London, 1967) Coghill also discerns a subterranean religious need in her, saying 'she obscurely felt some pull of Heaven's magnets, as well as the world's'. Several other critics also discern shadowy or hidden aspects of her character, so that in addition to Coghill's idea of religious yearnings, she is described as an unfulfilled poet, and A. C. Cawley, in his introduction to the Everyman *Canterbury Tales*, guesses that the discourse on 'gentillesse' reveals 'a submerged aspect of her nature'. In creating Alison, Chaucer 'got as near as he ever did to that "interior nature of humanity" . . . '

Finally, critics are divided on the question of how seriously we should take the Wife of Bath. To some she is light entertainment, providing knockabout comedy, and we should not read too much into her obvious immorality. Coghill, among others, sees 'tragedy' in her character and likens her to Shakespeare's Falstaff as a great tragi-comic creation.

Prologue and Tale

Another argument between critics concerns the style and suitability of the Tale. There are those who feel that the Tale is in a different vein, and could not have been told by Alison. For example James Winny (see pp. 51–2) is convinced that: 'By failing to marry its philosophical interests to the poetry of direct sensation, *The Wife's Tale* falls short.' According to Winny, Alison has been replaced by a 'courtly narrator', and the 'gentillesse' sermon is the most unlikely passage of all, for without it the Tale would have been 'disproportionately short, but altogether more plausible'. John Speirs disagrees. In his opinion, 'We continue to hear the Wife's voice in the telling of her mature tale of "fayerye" '. Nevill Coghill notices that 'the style changes' in the Tale, but sees the 'masterly' hand of Chaucer knitting together the Prologue and Tale into 'a notable example of Chaucer's skill in narrative'.

The marriage debate

The critics broadly agree that there is a theme of marriage, and the Wife of Bath contributes to a larger discussion in *The Canterbury Tales*. There the agreement ends. Again, the main controversy is between those who emphasise humanity and dramatic realism, and those who see Chaucer as a didactic poet. The former see Alison's discourse as a dramatic event in the story of the pilgrimage, provoking her audience and issuing a challenge on the subject of marriage. John Speirs writes that her Prologue and Tale 'introduce a succession of tales (evidently intended by Chaucer to stand together). Several of these present diverse attitudes to marriage and thus constitute a *debate* on this theme.' George Lyman Kittredge emphasises the audience of pilgrims, saying that her Prologue 'begins a new act in the drama', and he describes the Clerk's reaction as 'scandalized' to the point where he is 'roused to protesting answer' (see Further Reading under Wagenknecht). D. W. Robertson, on the other hand, dismisses the theatrical metaphor. In his view, marriage stands for order in society. In fourteenth-century philosophy, 'marriage' also described the relationship between humanity and God through the symbolism of baptism. Chaucer sets this theme, which stands for everything in the world, 'in humanistic terms in the Knight's Tale'. Robertson goes on: 'Once it is seen that the elaboration of the theme of marriage in the *Tales* is thematic rather than dramatic, the false problems raised by the old theory of the "marriage group" disappear.' In this view a woman usurping man's traditional authority in marriage is comparable to man usurping the authority of God, so the Wife represents chaos or the destruction of order.

As you can see, there is no shortage of argument among the critics. With a text so provocative, volatile and ambiguous there is a rich field for controversy, and each contribution on the subject, however different or argumentative it may seem, can help us to valuable insight when we are studying Chaucer. Like most artists in relation to their critics, he transcends them all.

REVISION QUESTIONS

These questions should act as a stimulus to consideration of different aspects of the text. They also suggest the range of topics that might be the focus of questions in an examination.

1. 'The Wife of Bath's Prologue is constructed more like a play than a narrative poem.' Examine Chaucer's use of dramatic devices in the Prologue and say how far you agree with this comment on the text.

2. 'Gentillesse? – She doesn't know what the word means!' Examine the theme of 'gentillesse' in the light of this opinion of Alison.

3. How far would you agree that 'maistrye' is the tragedy of Alison's life?

4. When the Pardoner calls Alison a 'noble prechour', do you think she most deserves his praise for her logic and learning, or her cunning ingenuity in argument?

5. With close reference to at least **three** different episodes, show what you consider to be the outstanding features of Chaucer's style in 'The Wife of Bath's Prologue and Tale'.

6. 'The woman who buffets us with the gusty story of her life could not have told this *Tale* – neither the content nor the style is conceivably that of Alison of Bath.' Comment in detail on this view of the relationship between Prologue and Tale.

7. 'No subtlety, no irony, but lots of blue jokes and raucous fun!' Is this a fair assessment of 'The Wife of Bath's Prologue'?

8. 'Oon of us two moste bowen, doutelees.' Choose any **two** of the marriages described in the text and say how far you think the truth of this line is demonstrated by Alison's 'experience'.

9. In discussing Alison of Bath's character, how far and in what sense should we take account of her claim that she is the victim of adverse astrological influences?

10. 'It makes girls deceitful and boys into chauvinists – The Wife of Bath's Prologue and Tale should be proscribed'. How far do you think the text encourages sexual stereotypes?

11. 'It is about the dreadful institution of marriage: it is a case history of social ills.' Explain what you think is gained and lost from looking at the Prologue and Tale in this light.

12. Examine the imagery of The Wife of Bath's Prologue and Tale, explaining how this contributes to the total effect.

13. 'Ordinary speech and poetry have rarely been in such harmony together'. Do you see this aspect of Chaucer's art as a major element in his creation of Alison of Bath?

14. 'Alison knows no more of love than the brutal rapist in her Tale'. Is this a fair comment on Alison's emotions and attitudes?

15. 'It is just so funny!' With close reference to at least **three** episodes, show how Chaucer creates and enhances comedy in the Wife's Prologue and Tale.

FURTHER READING

Chaucer's works

The standard edition of Chaucer's works is *The Works of Geoffrey Chaucer*, edited by F. N. Robinson (2nd edition, London: Oxford University Press, 1957). This gives an authoritative text of 'The Wife of Bath's Prologue and Tale' and contains a useful Glossary and detailed textual notes. Students not so familiar with Middle English, however, may prefer to read in A. C. Cawley's Everyman edition of the *Canterbury Tales* (London: J. M. Dent & Sons, 1958). This provides a modern synonym in the margin for difficult words, and paraphrases of difficult lines at the bottom of the page.

The first thing to do after reading 'The Wife of Bath's Prologue and Tale', is to read more widely in *The Canterbury Tales*. You should read 'The General Prologue' to gain a sense of the framework of the whole work, then I would suggest reading at least some of the so-called 'marriage' group of tales: 'The Clerk's Tale', 'The Merchant's Tale' and 'The Franklin's Tale'. With so much reading of Chaucer to undertake, you may wish to use Nevill Coghill's translation, published as *The Canterbury Tales* by Penguin Books (London, 1951); but, of course, no translation can match the original.

Criticism and commentaries

This list has been kept short, as it is only intended to provide a sample ranging across some different views. Most critical works give plentiful suggestions for further reading, so this list should be regarded merely as a start.

Anderson, J. J. (ed.) *Chaucer: The Canterbury Tales* (London: Macmillan, 1974).
This volume in the 'Casebook' Series contains a wide range of critical contributions.

Robertson, D. W., Jr, *A Preface to Chaucer* (London and Princeton N. J.: Oxford University Press, 1962). This enormously scholarly work can be invaluable in helping us to understand medieval ideas, and the commentary on the Wife's Prologue (pp. 317–31) is particularly worthy of attention.

Speirs, John, *Chaucer the Maker* (London: Faber and Faber, 1951). Commentary on the Wife of Bath is found on pp. 136–49.

Wagenknecht, Edward (ed.) *Chaucer: Modern Essays in Criticism* (New York: Oxford University Press, 1959). In this collection of essays, Walter Clyde Curry's 'The Wife of Bath', George Lyman Kittredge's 'Chaucer's Discussion of Marriage' and Henry Barrett Hinckley's 'The Debate on Marriage in *The Canterbury Tales*' are directly concerned with the Wife of Bath.